# My Bush Babies

# My Bush Babies

## Iris Anderson

### with Dennis Hancock

**M**

*To all those people who ought to get awards*

First published 1979 by
THE MACMILLAN COMPANY OF AUSTRALIA PTY LTD
107 Moray Street, South Melbourne 3205
6 George Place, Artarmon 2064

Associated companies in
London and Basingstoke, England
New York  Dublin  Johannesburg  Delhi

National Library of Australia
cataloguing in publication data
Anderson, Iris.
  My bush babies.

  ISBN 0 333 25237 3

  1. Animals. I. Hancock, Dennis, joint author.
  II. Title.

591'.0924

Set in 'Monotype' Garamond, Series 156 by
Dudley E. King, Melbourne
Printed in Hong Kong

# Contents

Her Majesty the Queen has been graciously pleased to bestow the British Empire Medal upon Mrs Iris Eleanor Anderson, of Bicton, Western Australia, for her meritorious service in the preservation of fauna in Western Australia.

She has undertaken at her suburban residence the care of sick, injured and orphaned wild life. The rehabilitation of these animals has been carried out entirely at her own expense and is due to the work and devotion she has unremittingly given at all hours of the day and night. Approximately one hundred animals each year have benefited from her efforts.

Mrs Anderson has become recognised as an authority on the correct methods of rearing and tending sick and injured kangaroos and other marsupials, her advice being constantly sought in these matters.

A conservationist in the most practical manner, Mrs Anderson is admired for her work by many animal lovers.

Australian New Year's Honours List 1971

# Foreword

It is very seldom, when you browse through the New Year's Honours List, that you come upon a recipient of the B.E.M. whom you think is worthy of the award. However, nobody more worthy of this honour can be found than Iris Anderson.

I vividly remember the first time I met her. I had arrived in Perth and naturally made a beeline for the zoo, to be shown around by my friend, Tom Spence, the director. When we had finished our tour he said to me, 'Do you want to meet somebody really extraordinary in animal conservation and see some lovely marsupials?' Naturally, I said I did, so we drove to Iris Anderson's house—a comparatively small one in a suburban area of Perth. When we stopped outside it, I thought Tom Spence was pulling my leg for I could not conceive, in a small house like that, how anyone could keep a collection of marsupials. However, as soon as Iris greeted us and ushered us into her living-room, I changed my views. On every chair and indeed in every place where they could be hung, were endless pullovers with their bottoms sewn up and their arms knotted together. Peering out of the neckholes were the wistful and engaging faces of innumerable baby kangaroos and wallabies, nearly all of them orphans—their parents having been victims of hit-and-run drivers. To see them hopping about the floor and then, alarmed, diving straight back into their jerseys was an absolutely enchanting sight. Then we went into the garden—an ordinary small suburban garden—and were almost instantly knee-deep in the bigger kangaroos and wallabies that lived there.

I was tremendously impressed at the dedication shown to these animals by Iris and her husband and I felt it such extremely worthwhile work to do, as I knew from my own experience that keeping a large number of baby and adult animals like this was no cheap business. I asked Iris how she managed, to which she gave me a classic reply: 'Well,' she said, 'you see, we don't drink and we don't smoke and we don't gamble, so we put all our spare money into these babies.'

I think readers of this book will be as enchanted with it as I have been and I am very flattered that Iris should have asked me to write this introduction. I hope that it will do much to aid the conservation work for marsupials in Australia.

*Gerald Durrell*
*Channel Islands*
*January 1979*

# How It All Started

My first love affair was with a goat.

Even as goats go, he was not particularly attractive. He was more than a little off-white, with a hint of mange here and there. He had only one horn, a sinful glint in his yellow eye and an aroma which kept everyone but me at a respectful distance, particularly downwind. To me, however, he was both Prince Charming and the road to ruin—or at least to a lifelong slavery as far as animals are concerned. A demanding but far from dull slavery, which has seen me falling into ponds and marooned on roofs attempting to save not-so-dumb 'victims', which almost cost my husband his life at the claws of a psychopathic kangaroo and which led to my meeting the Governor of Western Australia with no knickers on (me, not him).

Lucky the goat has a lot to answer for. He wandered into my life when I was ten and living near Manjimup, a small timber township in the bottom left-hand corner of Western Australia. I never knew where he came from. I heard a padding behind me on the dusty 5-kilometre track between home and the local bush school, looked around and there he was. He probably sensed that he had found a pushover and as usual he was right. My childhood had been punctuated by dogs, cats, guinea-pigs and, when their habits proved less than domesticated, by the protests of my long-suffering parents. However, a pet not merely flaunting a kind of scruffy, leery, sexiness but almost as big as myself . . . !

The next two months were ecstasy, Lucky took over the unkempt paddock adjoining our home and with complete self-assurance took me over too. He met his match in Mother when he tried to nudge his way into the kitchen, protesting loudly at the half-nelson which she got on his solitary horn, but to me he could do no wrong. I grew skinny both through adoration and through his complacent acceptance of all the smuggled-out meals which were meant for me.

Like most first loves, the end was tragedy and disillusion. It came when Dad bought tickets for one of the few live

9

shows which ventured so far into the bush—starring a magician, no less, the first that my three brothers and I had ever seen. Or did not see, thanks to Lucky.

Since he had first adopted me, he had taken it as his right that he should accompany me everywhere—mainly because he was sure of pocketsful of titbits on the way. He did not intend to change his routine for a little thing like a bush concert. Shutting him in the paddock, I bade him a sentimental goodnight as the family, stiffly dressed in its Sunday best, set off down the track for Manjimup. It was a waste of time and emotion, as he proved by galloping up behind us before we had gone more than a few hundred metres. We never found out how he was able to open a strongly-wired gate, but he was certainly an expert. We had to admit that when he skittered up for the third time, wearing a halo of dust and a contemptuous sneer.

Mother did not appreciate either. Slapping at the dust which coated her finery, she made it plain between sneezes that Lucky must be persuaded to stay home—or else. Pushing and pulling, my brother Leslie and I got him back to the paddock yet again and, in a panic, consulted on how to keep him there. Leslie spotted the apparent answer hanging on a stout nail outside the kitchen door: a huge, coffin-shaped zinc bath which, twice weekly, was dragged indoors and filled from a hot kettle so that in solemn order of priority we could each be dunked and scrubbed. This monster, we thought, should be just the thing to immobilize Lucky—particularly when he was linked to it by a chain from the barn heavy enough to flatten a whole shipload of galley-slaves.

Running hard, we overtook our disapproving parents and sniggering brothers, confident that we had solved the problem at last. Our complacency survived for about three minutes. Then it was shattered by a chorus of clatters and clanks which slowly but inexorably gained upon us. By now it was getting dusk and the effect was eerie in the extreme. We were exchanging looks of guilty horror on my part and mounting indignation on Mother's when Lucky appeared through the gloom. Behind him, like Ben Hur's chariot without wheels, bounded the almost bottomless bath. He overtook us still at the gallop, then braked with all four feet as he skidded to a halt alongside.

Several seconds later, Mother's face reappeared through

the resulting dust-cloud. Her expression was such that I rather wished it had not. I prefer not to recall her comments in detail. She had plenty of time to amplify them as we all trailed back to the house to shed our filthy finery and reconcile ourselves to the fact that it was far too late to get to the show.

This time, Lucky had overstepped the mark once and for all. He was gone the next morning. Although I longed to know what had happened to him, I had the sense to realize that it would be tactful and far less painful not to ask.

It is probably time I introduced myself.

I was born at Gravesend, Kent, but I cannot remember much about England—just ships in the Thames with the Downs behind and green, hedged fields very different from our parched Australian paddocks—since we sailed for Australia when I was very small. My mother's family was theatrical in every sense. Grandfather had been a member of the Mumming Birds troupe with the then unknown Charlie Chaplin, and Mother was actually in a few silent films before we decided to migrate. Migration ended her career, but only professionally. She remained an actress all her life, even though her only audience was her awe-stricken family. Apparently I raised her hopes of hereditary talent when, toddling home after a country excursion, I displayed an almost non-existent spot on my arm and announced, 'A butterfly kicked me!' But if this did indicate a gift for drama, as opposed to a riotous imagination, it must have withered under the Australian sun. Looking back, I am sure it was Mother's instinctive sense of melodrama which carried her through a good many very difficult years when she brought up the four of us with no help and very little money.

My father I remember as her exact opposite—a quiet, retiring man who had been trained as an electrician before his ill-fated efforts at farming in the bush. It is not surprising that he soon faded out of our lives and Mother took over as head of the family. The years that followed must have been very hard for her, particularly when, thanks to the Great Depression, her little store at Manjimup failed and she was forced to transplant all of us 250 kilometres north to the metropolitan port of Fremantle. It was a tremendous upheaval for my brothers and me. For years we had lived surrounded by some of the world's most spectacular forest—our horizons limited by karri trees often more than 70 metres high and so massive we could hold parties inside their hollow trunks. Fremantle seemed bare and bustling by comparison and even the fun of swimming and surfing in the unbelievably blue Indian Ocean did little to ease the sense of strangeness which we felt for the first few months.

However, I can never remember feeling that we were ever in really serious trouble. When crises occurred, as they did only too often, Mother's reaction was always so splendidly melodramatic that we watched with the fascinated appreciation of first-nighters instead of realizing that the problems were real. And the pleasure of an audience seemed to insulate her too from harsh reality. 'Desperate, but not serious' sums up the atmosphere of our childhood pretty well.

Much of this went over my head anyway because I was still involved with a constant succession of pets. After the ill-fated episode with Lucky I retreated for a time to my former dogs-and-cats routine. However, Mother was transformed into a raging Lady MacBeth when a pet possum which I had smuggled into bed amused himself after I had dropped off to sleep by clawing down the curtains, then climbing on to the dresser and methodically hurling every china ornament to the floor. The resulting series of crashes would have woken the dead. It certainly woke me and Mother who, in a flowing white nightie with her long hair streaming, put on one of the most impressive performances I had yet seen. The possum was banished forever from the house—not withstanding my entreaties and the fact that I had named it after her favourite screen hero, Douglas Fairbanks. Fairbanks-type athletics, I gathered, might be irresistible on the screen but not among the family knick-knacks.

# Me After Archie

I suppose it was inevitable that eventually my affections should be transferred to someone taller and rather less hairy than his predecessors. The victim's fate was sealed when I spotted him at a weekly dance at Fremantle Town Hall; so was mine.

Actually, there was no reason whatsoever to regard him as romantic. My escort and I had arrived fairly late in the evening and the lean, dark-haired chap partly blocking the foot of the stairs gave the distinct impression that he had spent the preceding few hours in a nearby hostelry. Apart from getting in the way, he was concentrating with apparent difficulty upon blowing up a pink balloon, then letting it down again with nasty if not obscene noises. But there was something about him . . .

I did not see him again for three weeks. In the meantime, I had cleared the decks for action by ending my tentative engagement. Then my chance came. I had finished my behind-the-counter shift at the local chain store and was waiting for a tram home when I saw the same lanky, relaxed figure propping up a nearby lamp-post. At almost the same time a pensioner who was a regular at the store wandered by and said 'G'day, miss'. That is, he intended to wander by. I had never before exchanged greater intimacies with him than 'Here's your change', but he found himself cornered and talked at with a determination which would have made the Ancient Mariner seem like a deaf mute by comparison. I made certain that the bewildered old gentleman had his back to my target; he really did look like—to use a bit of picturesque Australiana—a stunned mullet. Whenever he glanced sideways in search of escape, I semaphored desperately with my eyebrows to the lamp-post lounger 20 metres away.

I still feel ashamed of such low cunning. It took a while to work, but then exactly what I hoped for happened. The watching figure straightened itself by degrees, detached itself from the post and sauntered slowly but meaningfully up behind my victim. The first intimation he had of its presence was a slow drawl, good-natured on the whole but with a slight edge of menace, which asked, 'Is this feller annoying you, love?'

I suppose the question should really have been flattering to an old chap who had topped his three-score and ten, but he obviously found it the last straw. He gave an upward glance at the questioner, a deservedly dirty look at me and took off, his stick tapping an indignant tattoo—while I, eyelashes working overtime, gazed at my 'rescuer' in adoration which was only temporarily speechless.

I cannot pretend the effect was overwhelming, or quick. We stood talking for what seemed hours and probably was about the weather (which is so uniformly perfect in Fremantle it provides a poor topic), about the store and about East Fremantle's chances on Saturday against its footy arch-rivals, Perth. I thought my ankles would snap and even when it came, the result was not remarkable for its eager gallantry. 'I'll walk you home if you like,' was just what I had been praying for, but it seemed to lose something when he added, 'as long as you don't live very far' . . .

Fortunately, I didn't. Even so, I managed to spin out the short stroll to another hour—not just because my feet hurt, but to provide more time to impress him. I told him about my English background, embroidering horribly and hinting at distinguished ancestry on the wrong side of the blanket, I promoted Mother to a scintillating star of the silver screen who now lived in Western Australia only to avoid her hordes of fans in Britain and America, then, fearful that I was overdoing the glamour in her favour, I hinted meaningfully that not only did I drink and smoke but Mother let me stay out all night . . .

For once, she might have been proud of my acting ability, but things did not work out that way. Just as Archie (a lovely name, I had decided immediately) was about to respond to this catalogue of enlightenment and easy virtue, we found ourselves at my front gate. Before I even had time to decide whether he was likely to kiss me, a window crashed open and an outraged voice, throbbing with emotion and maternal fears, demanded full-throatedly, 'Iris! Who is that man—and what are you doing staying out after ten o'clock?'

Mother had stolen the limelight again, not that Archie

stopped to see. It took me three weeks to catch up with him, but I have still got him.

The war was really responsible for our animal build-up. It broke out soon after we got married and just as we were planning to buy a government-built house in Bicton, on the south bank of the Swan River between Fremantle and Perth.

Archie joined the Army and I reacted with true wifely fortitude by drenching the Government housing representative in tears and asking what was the point of buying a house since the man who should be about it was certain to be killed serving his country. The Government chap was either a psychologist or a cynic, probably both. He wiped himself down and pointed out that if I was determined to devote the rest of my life to being a grief-stricken war widow, I could do it much more comfortably in a place of my own. So we bought and never regretted it. It was a pleasant little house with a pleasant garden, ideal for the collection of dogs and cats with which I surrounded myself to compensate for Archie's absence. Other people noticed my animal family and began to ask advice on how to cure their own pets' minor ills or repair the damage done by fights. There was no indication then just how inadequate that suburban quarter-acre would become. Within a few years it was crowded enough to make Noah's Ark seem like an empty supertanker.

And Archie? The worst war injury he got was a broken arm when an army truck turned over one night about 15 kilometres from home. In fact, he was the only one hurt—because, he claims, he was the only sober occupant. I believe him, naturally.

# Little Nell

My first kangaroo was the orphan of a murder victim. So young that she was still completely hairless, she had never even left her mother's pouch before her mother was killed by a party of self-styled 'hunters' on a weekend trip out of Perth with the usual equipment of army surplus rifles, several crates of beer and an old utility truck with a spot-light to dazzle its prey.

There may be arguments in favour of keeping kangaroo numbers down by professional thinning-out, although, as kangaroos were first by several thousand years, I can never really see why they should be slaughtered to make way for domestic stock. In any case, weekenders are not in it for anything but selfish reasons. Not merely selfish, but sadistic. How else can you describe men who will slaughter com-pletely defenceless animals by chasing them until they are at the point of collapse, training a spotlight which holds them mesmerized with fear and then riddling them from close range as a sitting target?

Fortunately, there are a number of would-be 'hunters' whose stomachs rebel as soon as they find out just what is involved. Among them was the young man who arrived on our doorstep with Nellie stuffed inside his ex-army camou-flage smock. He had set out the day before with a bunch of old hands, all agog at the prospects of a 'safari'. The first night's shooting had left him shocked and horrified—particularly at the fate of the baby kangaroos, or joeys, whose brains were dashed out against the nearest tree. 'I'm off hunting for life', he told me. And, as an effort to make amends, he had smuggled Nellie away from the slaughter and brought her to me to save.

I do not know how he had heard about our budding menagerie—and I am certain he did not realize just how misplaced his faith was. What I knew about marsupials could have been comfortably written on the back of a postage stamp. Like most people in Australia, I regarded them with a kind of sentimental patriotism; wasn't it obliging (and wise) of the Almighty to recognize what a special breed Australians were by sending us such a special,

These four joeys, now between 7–9 months old, were only babies when found in the pouches of kangaroos which had been shot by hunters.

if slightly ridiculous, animal? To me they were cuddly symbols rather than actual living individuals and, as I was to find out, they do not come any more individual than kangaroos . . .

My first shock was when her conscience-stricken protector drew her slowly and carefully out of his smock. To my astonished gaze, she seemed endless. First, a rat-like tail and an interminable pair of spindly legs, with tiny three-toed feet and very knobbly elbows; then a skinny pink-and-grey body, pear-shaped like those toys you can't knock over and so naked it made you blush to look at it; then, a small head with ridiculously big ears and round dark eyes with an expression so terrified and helpless that it wrung my heart.

I did the wrong thing immediately. Realizing that she had had no food since her mother's death the previous night, I warmed some pasteurized cows' milk, put it in a baby's bottle, put the teat to Nellie's mouth and waited complacently for her to suck it dry. Poor little love, she certainly tried. She could smell the milk and even taste the little that dribbled out, but the teat was so much bigger than her mouth that her nose was flattened against its end and she could neither suck nor draw breath. Forced into using my head, I searched desperately for a teat which was more to scale. Where on earth, in a household not noted for its handyman aspect, could I find a rubber mouthpiece small enough for Nellie?

It is amazing what providence will come up with—even if it is a bit painful at the time. In my scuttling around, I cornered too sharply on the verandah and found myself nursing a gashed shin with my son's bicycle on top of me. Pleased that said son was not home to hear some very un-maternal language, I attempted to lift off the infernal machine. Then the haze of agony cleared and I found myself gazing, at a range of 15 centimetres, at the answer to my (and Nellie's) problem. A tyre valve . . .!

It took a few minutes to bind up my throbbing leg and to find out how to remove the valve. Eventually, it came unscrewed with an explosive hiss like a space rocket and hurled itself across the verandah to disappear into the

---

Iris feeds her orphaned joeys a mixture of full cream powdered milk with a vitamin additive and a little cornflour.

unmown lawn. Five minutes later I found it, peeled off the rubber core and rushed back to Nellie. Brain now functioning feverishly, for she seemed visibly weaker, I heated a needle, bored out the baby's teat with it and stuck the valve rubber through the resulting hole. It worked. The valve rubber fitted snugly into the joey's mouth (it was, I found out later, not unlike the size and shape of a kangaroo's nipple). With most unladylike slurps and an expression of absolute bliss, she emptied the bottle in no time at all. Then she fell asleep, still dribbling, in the 'kangaroo pouch' I had contrived from an old woollen jumper and a hot-water bottle.

For four days everything went beautifully, then the trouble started. Quite suddenly Nellie began to vomit back every bottleful, her obvious distress increased by heavy scouring. Soon, she was refusing to drink at all. As she grew thinner and weaker, her eyes seemed bigger and more pleading. She was so utterly dependent and I was growing frantic . . .

I did what I should have done in the first place and rang our local vet, Phil Harwood. Fortunately, he took a great interest in marsupials—and almost burst my eardrum when he heard how much milk I was tipping into Nellie.

'125 millilitres every four hours?—my God, you'll pop the poor little devil!' he roared down the telephone. 'Cut that to 30 millilitres and not pasteurized. What she needs is milk straight from the cow . . .'

I pointed out gently that this was a bit difficult when we lived in a metropolitan suburb. Eventually we compromised on full-cream powdered milk with a vitamin additive and a little cornflour to give it body. Nellie took an experimental slurp and perked up in no time at all. From that time she never looked back. In a few weeks she had quadrupled her size, her lovely grey fur had grown and she was a very svelte young lady indeed.

No longer content to stay in her 'pouch', she spent much of her time investigating the garden, practising her hops on the lawn and showing off to admiring visitors. But she was still a baby at heart. If I was out of her sight for long, I would hear the odd little cough—a sort of self conscious 'ahem' which she used to attract my attention. Then, when I appeared, she would hop close and look up appealingly, to be lifted in my arms and snuggle down to sleep.

# Pestilential Possums

When we adopted Nellie we had no idea what a momentous step we were taking. In fact, it proved the point of no return. From then on we were branded as amiable eccentrics who would always be happy to take in lame dogs, lame ducks or any other kind of creature in trouble. The path which was consequently beaten to our door has seen increasingly heavy traffic ever since.

In fact, our next adoptee was lame and a traffic victim. Freddy the possum was found on a nearby highway with a broken leg and a concussion. In no time I was again in consultation with our friendly (if irascible) neighbourhood vet. It is a wonder more possums are not involved in over-civilized mishaps like being hit by cars. They are far too fond of urban life, both for their own good and for the tempers of their involuntary hosts. Nothing is more lovable and cuddly than a possum, except perhaps a koala—and nothing is more infuriating than the midnight creaks and scrabbles that mean one, or more probably a family, has decided to take up residence in your roof-space. By day, even in heavily populated areas, possums are almost impossible to spot. By night, when you are trying vainly to sleep, their presence is very obvious indeed . . .

But Freddy, no matter what his former peccadilloes, was such a charmer that we fell for him as soon as we saw him.

The bright eyes peering up from his travelling box brightened still further when I fed him a handful of rose petals—for possum tastes, as befit those of a town-dweller, are so sophisticated as to verge on the kinky. He behaved beautifully while his leg was set, which encouraged me to reach in and pat him. That was my first mistake.

Freddy, it proved, was quite happy to be fed and doctored, but did not regard that as an excuse for mere humans to take liberties. After all, possums were penthouse-dwellers, and as such much too high in the social scale to mix with any member of the proletariat who felt so in-clined . . . He made his views known in no uncertain fashion by giving me a nip on the thumb which sent me, hand tucked into blouse like a Women's Lib Napoleon, racing for the medical cabinet. While I bound up my throbbing thumb, Freddy watched with such complacency that I only just resisted the temptation to tip his water-bowl right over his head. However, he taught me a valuable lesson. Animals, very sensibly, remain on the defensive until they are quite sure that humans are to be trusted completely—for Freddy, a bandaged leg and a few rose petals did not yet constitute a lifetime friendship.

After that I resorted to age-old feminine hypocrisy and, ostensibly at least, left all the approaches to him. It worked like a charm. Either my coyness aroused his romantic instinct or piqued his male vanity, because in no time at all he was quite shamelessly giving me the eye. The final proof came when, having gingerly inspected his healing leg, he tested it with a sudden leap on to my shoulder and peered soulfully into my face like a second-rate Valentino. Even when he was well enough to take up residence in the huge cage which Archie built around an old garden gum tree, he would still use all his charm to entice me in there with him. Once inside, he would snuggle shamelessly, play with my hair, do everything in fact except invite me to inspect his etchings.

Only one thing kept my own vanity in check. I could not fail to notice that his welcome was just a little less ecstatic and his courting technique just a little more offhand if I did not bring with me an apple, a handful of nuts or dates or a bar of milk chocolate. Like a good many of his two-legged counterparts, the way to Freddy's heart went more smoothly with a detour through his stomach . . .

Actually, that is hardly fair to Freddy. Somebody did reach his heart in a much more convincing way that I did and certainly not by cosseting him. In fact Freda, apart from being a possum, was a perfect little bitch and completely unimpressed by his soulful charm. She was brought in shivering and miserable, an obvious pneumonia victim. I was delighted when we pulled her through, envisaging an idyllic, bright-eyed family with Freddy and Freda as proud parents and myself as doting grandma. The sentimental dream was shattered on what I was already referring to in Ethel M. Dell fashion as The First Night.

Freda, now recovered enough for a little amorous dalliance, had been slipped into Freddy's cage a few hours earlier with two handfuls of nuts and raisins as a wedding feast. They were still tucking into it when I tactfully withdrew. I climbed into bed beside Archie and discoursed on the delights of young love until a muffled snore told me I was wasting my breath. I was just dozing off myself when what to my bemused mind sounded like World War III broke out, apparently just outside the window. A series of tremendous bangs was followed by spitting, howling and screeching which made the average tomcat's melee seem like a vicarage tea-party by comparison. Freddy, it was obvious, had just got around to putting the hard word on his bride and was receiving much harder ones in return.

By then, Archie too had rebounded from the bedroom ceiling. His comments on my matchmaking, or what I could hear of them above the din, were quite unprintable. His attitude did not mellow during the next few days and neither did that of Freda. By day, the newlyweds sulkily ignored each other, but this seemed merely an interlude to lick their wounds and gather strength for the next affray. Every night was made hideous by their bumps and yells, and by Archie's indignant roars as he buried his head under the pillow. Consequently, we were stunned beyond description a few weeks later when, examining Freda's latest conjugal scars, I saw a tiny black face with enormous eyes peering from her pouch. Evidently she and Freddy had not been fighting *all* the time . . .

If I imagined Fran, in classic agony-column fashion, would bring her parents closer together I was speedily disillusioned. The fighting continued unabated. I was worried stiff that Fran, still confined to Freda's pouch, would develop terrible psychological traumas even if she did not become permanently punch-drunk. Yet, in three months, Freda produced Ferdi and a love-and-war pattern was established which soon presented us with yet another problem. The trouble was that the children took after their parents. As soon as they were old enough, fighting and fornicating, as Archie so elegantly put it, became the order of the day. By a process of multiplication and compound interest, in every sense, we found ourselves refereeing the bouts and staunching the wounds of fifteen battle-scarred, sex-mad possums. It could not go on of course. The neighbours, though they obviously regarded our establishment as a cross between Madison Square Garden and

Hugh Hefner's penthouse, were surprisingly good about both types of banging. It was Archie and I, not to mention the other animals, who could not stand the strain.

Our saviour was Harry Butler, a self-taught Perth naturalist who has since become famous beyond Australia for his conservation efforts and his remarkable animal insight. Our garden was a perpetual battleground, he explained, for a classic reason—lack of *lebensraum*. Every adult possum stakes a claim to its own tree and will fight off all intruders. If we wanted to keep fifteen possums, it seemed we should have to plant fifteen more trees. As the possums would undoubtedly multiply much quicker than the trees grew, the whole concept just was not on. Harry, having pinpointed the problem, also had the answer. He knew of a patch of bush not too far from Perth which not only had spare trees for possums, but plenty of water and natural food. So, with heavy hearts, we decided to keep Freddy and one female (not Freda, whose temper had gone from bad to horrible) and to liberate the rest on their new housing estate.

It was not that easy, of course. Nothing about those possums ever was. We loaded them, wrestling and scratching, into individual boxes while Archie's swearing competed with theirs for the last time. Having piled the boxes and their infuriated contents into the back of our station wagon, we set off to the woods. Careful planning was needed even there. Acting on Harry's instructions, we checked each tree carefully for the bark scratchings indicating a possum was already in residence until we had sorted out thirteen 'empty' trees. Around the bole of each, we scattered nuts and raisins to make the possums feel at home. Then we carried a box to each tree, opened it and waited for the possums' ecstatic gratitude for having found them all highly desirable residences with all mod. cons. and rent-free. But our awkward squad was awkward to the last. Each possum came out of its box, surveyed its tree, then fixed us with a contemptuous eye which said as plainly as words, 'If *you* want to move to the bush that's OK by us, but don't expect us to become country hicks.' Then, with one accord, they scuttled back to the car. Archie and I were last in the rush and there was not even room for us to get in.

It should have been funny, but it wasn't. Pests though

they were, I felt like a traitor as we discussed how to desert them, even though it was for their own good. Eventually, after taking them back to their respective trees, I talked to them while Archie headed back to the car. Then he turned the radio on full to deter them, slipped into gear and rolled the car forward as I sprinted over and hurled myself into the seat beside him. I looked back to see every possum sitting up and staring after us as we drove away. I cried. I couldn't help it.

A few weeks later we went back and found every tree belonging to 'our' possums had the bark scratching which indicated that the townies had settled in. It was obvious that we had done the right thing. But even now, all these years after, I cannot think about it without feeling guilty.

# More Marsupials

Before we get further involved with dotty animals and dotty names, it might be as well to explain that Australia has almost as many kinds of marsupials as the rest of the world has of more conventional animals.

Some are in fact remarkably similar. The marsupial tiger —which is now extinct on the mainland but which, some of us believe, still lives in the impenetrable 'horizontal' bush of Western Tasmania—was or is a big, carnivorous marsupial with stripes. The Tasmanian Devil is a tubby, scrubby, not very endearing beast which looks and behaves very much like a wild boar, while the marsupial mouse is just as cuddly, or as scary, as his European counterpart.

Kangaroos, of course, could hardly be mistaken for anything overseas. But they themselves, together with their cousins the wallabies, muster at least twenty varieties. Some are big, some are comparatively tiny, some are gracefully built, some are rather chunky, some have grey woolly fur, some have straight, glossy hair of a beautiful chestnut red and some can be surprisingly fierce. I know professionals at the Perth Zoo who are quite happy about going into lions' and tigers' cages but would not dream of being alone with one big, aggressive 'roo whose out-lashing, razor-sharp hooves could disembowel a man in seconds. Fortunately, there are not many like that.

On the other hand, I cannot help feeling a sneaking admiration for a kangaroo which got the better of a poll shorthorn bull. It happened a few years ago on a property near York, about 130 kilometres east of Perth, when a farmer turned his pet 'roo loose in the same paddock as the bull. No doubt he thought 5 hectares was big enough for the two to share, but the bull had other ideas. He demonstrated them promptly by trotting across the paddock and tossing the 'roo, Little Joe. This first toss was a moderate one, but when Little Joe failed to take the hint the bull tossed him again—a distance which the awestruck farmer, Mr Fred Robinson, later measured from the dust-marks as about 5 metres. With that the bull, having made

It is common for kangaroos to produce offspring of a different colour
to themselves. This tammar, one of the smaller varieties, is seen here
with her albino offspring.

its point, put its nose in the air, bellowed triumphantly and trotted away. Mr Robinson was about to enter the paddock and rescue his pet, but he under-estimated Little Joe. Before the farmer could grab him he climbed to his feet, leapt after the bull and proceeded to clobber it with upward kicks from his strong hind legs like a French boxer gone berserk. It was the bull which eventually retreated— to a far corner of the paddock, from which he refused to budge until Little Joe was led away. Mr Robinson found him other quarters. 'Not to protect Little Joe,' he said later, 'just that I didn't want my prize stud bull terrorized into impotence by a fighting-mad marsupial.'

One of the biggest and most beautiful species of kangaroo is the red, or Marloo—but immediately we hit more than a bit of confusion. The bucks can in fact be fawn-coloured, while the does are often a lovely shade of soft blue-gray. In our sanctuary we can muster at the same time one blue doe with a red joey in her pouch, a bright red doe with a fawn joey and a splendid golden doe whose offspring matches her exactly. If Australians tend to be a bit colour-conscious, their animals certainly are not!

One thing Marloos have in common—a woolly coat and black-and-white facial markings. This distinguishes them from the Great Grey kangaroo. Like the Marloo, these can reach a height of 180 centimetres or more and the noise of their 130 kilograms bounding across rock-hard ground justifies well their slang-name of boomers. Great Greys have a short thick pelt of light grey. So do Coastal Greys, whereas the Forester has a darker pelt and a deer-like face.

The stocky Euros have heads more like donkeys. Varying from greyish fawn to deep red, they have hair instead of fur and thick muscley arms which can squeeze an attacker into complete helplessness. The Agile Wallaby from northern Australia is smaller but also has strong arms with long curved nails.

My favourites are the Black-Gloved Wallabies, which live in forest areas. Only about 50 centimetres tall, they are delicately built, with big brown eyes and incredibly long thick lashes to protect them as they bound through the spiky undergrowth. Their dark grey pelt is soft and silky

---

The stocky euros have a head more like a donkey's and hair instead of fur which varies from greyish-fawn to deep red.

and they take their name from the close, neatly groomed fur which covers their tiny front paws like black velvet. When they hold a titbit between their gloves and nibble it daintily; it is exactly like Great Aunt Agatha come to tea . . .

Even smaller than these are marsupials with such unlikely names as tammars, damars, numbats and quokkas. Quokkas are now almost extinct except on Rottnest Island off Fremantle. Conservation laws stipulate that they must never be moved from there, which once involved me in a very embarrassing episode indeed. More of that later.

Possums were once described by a bemused pioneer as 'a cross between a small fox and a large dormouse'. There are more than twenty varieties, including the green ringtail whose fur actually is green from a type of algae which thrives on it. Even so, he is a lovable character—all possums are except the striped possum, which not only has markings exactly like a skunk but can emit a smell just as disgusting. If his best friends do tell him, he evidently takes no notice.

Wombats are pretty endearing too. I always think of them as the Australian equivalent of badgers—living in big burrows, amiable and vague-looking, they wander slowly about like absent-minded professors. But their looks are deceptive; if the need arises, they are very tough scrappers indeed. So are the marsupial cats, which look like European wildcats except that they are spotted instead of striped. Their usual prey is birds, but they will stand up to dogs and are quite capable of killing the smaller wallabies. On the other hand, they will not tackle echidnas, the ant-eaters which are as prickly as hedgehogs but are prized as good tucker by the Aborigines who roast them whole.

Some marsupials get a bit above themselves. There are kangaroos which live in trees and possums which actually 'fly' by extending the membranes which link their front and back legs. The koala is high in every sense. Not only does he never descend to ground level, but the eucalyptus leaves on which he is hooked keep him permanently good-natured but dopey—the hippy of the forest. His unchanging diet contains enough prussic acid to kill most animals. The only effect on the koala is to keep his coat clear of fleas.

---

A very tame and affectionate black-gloved wallaby with her joey. These delicately-built wallabies take their name from the black, velvet-like fur which covers their front paws.

Adorable little quokkas like this one are almost extinct on Rottnest
Island off the coast of W.A. They were mistaken for rats by the
Dutch sailors who were the first Europeans ashore in W.A.

32

Bandicoots could be called marsupial rabbits (as though we haven't got enough of *them*!) but the platypus defies comparison with anything else in the world and probably out of it. It must have caused quite a reaction at the Court of St James when the first antipodean explorers sent back stories of a cross between an otter and a farmyard duck. No wonder Aussies have had a reputation as con-men ever since!

# Traffic Orphans

Kangaroos have two great enemies. The first is that army of so-called sportsmen I have already mentioned who, partly for 'fun' and partly to make money from pet-food manufacturers, have already brought some species to the verge of extinction. The other enemy is the car. Kangaroos, sad to say, must be among the world's worst jay-walkers; not just those in the outback where cars may still be rare, but those near towns (and there are still more than you might think) which must have grown up almost within sound of the main road traffic streams. They are rarely seen during the day as they avoid the heat by nestling well down in the shady undergrowth, but in the early evening they rouse to forage for food and it is then that the trouble starts.

It is no fun for the motorist when, without any warning, a big 'roo hops from roadside scrub directly into the path of his car. A lot of expensive panel-beating is the inevitable result. There are quite a few stories of petrified drivers who find themselves with a shattered windscreen and an unwanted passenger beside them in the front seat. Such accidents are infuriating or a bit of a giggle, depending upon whether they happen to you or to someone else, but for the kangaroo concerned they are often fatal.

The situation is even more sad if there is a joey in the pouch. Nothing is more helpless or vulnerable than a baby kangaroo which is exposed to the dangers and discomforts of the outside world while the luckier offspring of conventional mammals can look forward to several months' more snuggling in the warmth and protection of the womb. The poor little joey is evicted only thirty-three days after conception—a naked, quivering scrap less than 2.5 centimetres long which looks more like a pink slug than an animal. Its first Herculean task is to climb up the outside of the pouch to the lip, unaided except for the path through her fur which the mother licks for it. The near-embryo is so undeveloped that it must remain for another eight months or so in the pouch and suckles for six months after that before it is able to look after itself.

Consequently, I had no real hope at all for the little traffic victim brought to us late one night by the young girl driver of the car which had killed its mother. The almost hairless joey was so young that its eyes were still just blue shadows under the pink skin. As soon as we took it gently from the coat in which it had been wrapped, it gasped and fell limp and motionless. The poor little mite was obviously dead, but the girl was so distressed that, merely to put on an act for her sake, I lifted the little body to my mouth and went through the motions of oral resuscitation. It really was nothing more than a gesture, to delay the moment when I would have to tell its rescuer her trouble in bringing it to us was in vain. Consequently, I could not believe it when, after a few minutes, the tiny scrap between my hands gave a shudder, a wriggle and then some quite definite pants! Astounded, I continued the treatment until the joey's breathing became normal. Its rescuer's gratitude was embarrassing, but in fact the baby (which proved to be a doe) was still not out of the wood. It took another month's feeding with an eyedropper before she was even developed enough to suck from a teat, but she had already proved so determined to live that I had no real fears for her survival. In fact, after that month she progressed by leaps and bounds (appropriate enough, I suppose, for a kangaroo). She is still with us ten years later—probably the only one of her species ever to have been saved by the kiss of life.

Another of our traffic orphans was far less co-operative. She was a euro doe we called Jedda after the heroine of a film about Aborigines. This may have given our infant an inflated ego, because she proved as arrogant as she was tiny. No matter how hard I tried to persuade her to feed, she would stiffen in my arms, twist her face away from the rubber teat and glare straight at me with an expression of pure hatred.

'I don't want you, I want my mother', it seemed to say. 'I don't know what has happened to her, but it's all your fault—and don't *dare* to think you could ever take her place.'

It was heartbreaking and I began to think her stubbornness—and her courage—would certainly kill her. There seemed just one chance of saving the little rebel; instead of continuing my vain efforts to soften her up by cuddles, I

decided to try a little amateur psychology. I put a playpen near the kitchen fire, dumped her inside and ignored her. When it was feeding time for the other joeys, I brought them next to the playpen, sat on the hearthrug and fed them there. For a while, Jedda's nose remained, metaphorically speaking, in the air. Then, from the corner of my eye, I saw it begin to twitch a little at the smell of warm milk. Eventually she hopped over to the edge of the playpen and slowly approached me. But when I turned and said, 'Hello, what do you want?' she retreated smartly again. As long as she played hard to get, so could I. I carried on feeding the rest of the family and ignored her. I had almost given up hope and was concentrating on feeding the last and littlest, when I felt a touch on my arm. There was Jedda—still trying to look defiant, but so pathetic and lost that I could not keep up my don't-care act any longer. I grabbed her, tucked her into one of our stock woollen pouches and nursed and crooned over her like a baby. For a moment she stiffened up again, but then I felt her relax. I held her in the crook of my left arm with my hand over her eyes, then I forced open her jaws, still clenched a little as though by habit, and put the rubber teat into her mouth. It was one of the most tender moments of my life when she began to suck.

She was obviously almost starved. Once started, she was ravenous and that first bottleful disappeared in near-record time. I cuddled her close until she dropped off to sleep. It was a different Jedda the next morning. As soon as I came into the kitchen, she was out of her pouch and pleading to be lifted up. She is a bit too big to lift now, but we have been inseparable ever since.

---

Jedda, a euro doe, is probably the only kangaroo to have been saved by the kiss of life. She is still with the Andersons twenty-one years later.

# Queer Folk

By now, news of our zany little zoo at Bicton had spread to an embarrassing extent. In fact, we were not a zoo—just a kind of unofficial animal clinic. The difference was that most of our patients had no real owners—just well-wishers who found them injured, brought them in and left them—consequently we found ourselves building up a sizeable stock of animals who were now fighting fit (often quite literally) but had nowhere to go.

The problem multiplied itself. To prevent the animals getting on to the road, Archie, now in the police force, spent his off-duty shifts building a kangaroo-proof fence around the garden. A fence high and sturdy enough to pen in a champion jumper like a 'roo is itself pretty unusual and became a feature of the neighbourhood. This too helped to spread the word. At one stage we were even a port-of-call for tourist coaches, whose passengers would stream out to Ooh and Aah over our varied collection of lodgers. Most of these had no objection at all. As any professional zoo-keeper knows, a surprising number of animals, far from being shy, really appreciate an audience. Kangaroos in particular love playing to the gallery—in in spite of their long lashes and coy expression they are the world's biggest extroverts with not a shy bone in their bodies.

Unfortunately, things began to get a little out of hand. The reason, as usual, was that small but poisonous proportion of people who spoil things for everyone else. I had reconciled myself to the fact that my garden as such was virtually doomed and did not really mind strangers tramping all over it. In a misguided effort to bring the human and animal species closer together, I even stripped my two almond trees of their nuts and kept these available for visitors to feed to the animals. I gave that up, disillusioned and angry, when some animals became sick and I found

A little grey joey standing patiently while his dressing is changed.

that visitors had been feeding them the shells while eating the nuts themselves.

There were other unhappy incidents when people somehow got the idea that we were running a business, not a sanctuary. Archie opened the door one day to a polite caller who asked if he could buy a kangaroo. We explained that money did not enter into it—we were only too happy if our young or disabled kangaroos could go to good homes where they would be well cared for and protected. But he seemed a nice chap, so Archie asked him how much he knew about 'roos and whether he had kept one as a pet before.

'Pet?—Not likely!' said the caller, an expression of some distaste flitting across his features. 'I want one as a gimmick. I'm a photographer and I thought if I had a kangaroo on a collar and chain and took it down to Fremantle to meet incoming liners, tourists would fall over themselves to be photographed with it. I reckon I'd make quids . . .'

We told him, I hope politely, that we did not fancy being party to a scheme that would terrify and demean an animal and we certainly would not let one go to anyone who regarded it as a kind of theatrical prop instead of a living creature. He was still bewildered and slightly indignant when Archie showed him the door.

Another incident was rather more unpleasant. A joey was brought in looking very poorly indeed. Its mother had fallen to a hunter's gun but that did not account for the little one's condition—very nearly starved, with two broken ribs, damage to both 'arms' and a dislocated tail which indicated it had been dragged around by that sensitive appendage. It was brought in by a European migrant, the mother of the children to whom the joey had been given. I wanted to ask how the poor little thing came to be in such a state but I had no chance. She merely pushed the bedraggled bundle at me, said 'Fix it—I want it back when it is better' and disappeared abruptly around the corner.

I was too concerned about the baby to follow her. A closer look revealed it was in even worse condition than first impressions indicated. Apart from the physical damage, its face and neck were caked into spikes which were so stiff that it could not move its head without pricking itself. In fact, it looked more like one of those spiny little lizards the kids call mountain devils, than a soft-furred animal. Most of the painful mess had obviously been there for weeks, but when I examined what looked at first like yellow pus under its chin, it proved to be sweetened condensed milk. Fortunately the joey had rejected this diet, for sugar is lethal to an immature kangaroo. But evidently the 'owners' had either been annoyed by what they regarded as mere stubbornness, or were too uncaring to think of an alternative. Instead, they had squeezed the milk at it from a tube until it had crystallized and solidified into a kind of agonizing helmet. It took hours to soak and wipe off the mess and even then I did not think it would recover. We were amazed as well as delighted when, slowly, its bones knit again and a diet of boiled rice-water and vitamin drops transformed it into a bright-eyed inquisitive imp unrecognizable as the half-dead waif of six weeks before.

There was one major snag—the woman who had brought it. I had assumed that she would be too ashamed ever to come back, but I was wrong. I answered a knock on the door one morning to be confronted by the same implacable face and the abrupt request, 'Want kangaroo back now'. I had not the slightest intention of returning the joey to the sort of treatment which had almost killed it before. With no guilt feeling whatsoever, I told her a flat lie and said the baby had died—knowing she was not the type to grieve over this. She didn't, but instead she got very angry indeed. Her face grew red, her fists beat the air as she tried to put into English exactly what she thought of me. Fortunately, no doubt, I could not understand all that she said. But I did gather, through the torrent of invective, that things would go ill for me if I did not give her another 'roo to replace the one I had 'killed' and when I refused to do this, she took off like a rocket surrounded by fizzing Latin imprecations.

I had tried to put up a stout front, but I must admit the nasty little scene had upset me. I was just settling down to a soothing cup of tea when I heard a car screech into the drive and saw through the window that my visitor was back—with reinforcements. The car seemed stuffed with angry people of whom the largest and angriest of all was obviously her husband. When he added his *basso profundo* to his wife's non-stop screeching falsetto, my own efforts to reply were drowned out completely. In any case, there seemed nothing new to say for I had no intention of giving up the joey. I retired inside, but this merely added fuel to the flames. There was a thunderous knocking on the door and even louder chorus as the rest of the car-load added its incomprehensible condemnations to the threats of the deprived couple in the star roles.

I really was getting seriously worried and looking for something to wedge under the door handle in true threatened-heroine fashion when the din outside stopped with uncanny suddenness. Then, after perhaps three seconds' silence, the car's engine roared, the gears grated horribly in reverse and gravel thrown by spinning tyres rattled against the window. I peered out timidly to see the car lurching violently as it tore out of the driveway and, in the foreground, the bewildered figure of my husband.

'What in Pete's name is going on?' he asked aggrievedly as I fell untidily into his arms. 'I stopped the car outside because I could see this other job blocking the driveway, got out to ask them whether they would mind moving it and before I could say a word, they took off like a bat out of hell and nearly ran me down on the way . . .'

Half-hysterical, I told him about our unwanted visitors and how glad I was that he had come off shift just at the right time and had not changed out of his uniform before coming home. Even if they don't know it, in an emergency our policemen are wonderful.

# Beetling About

The career–hobby we have had thrust upon us is certainly good for the soul because, whether you like it or not, it keeps you so utterly humble. Several times a week you are reminded how little you know and the culprits are usually children. To them, you are not an expert unless you know everything about every creature, which results in some very strange requests indeed.

One of them involved probably our smallest patient to date, brought to the door by a heartbroken five-year-old with tears still smudging his face. 'It's been run over', he wailed, and when I dashed towards the gate he added with rising desperation, 'No, *here* . . .' He opened his hand to reveal one of those tiny, glossy, sluggish creatures like a miniature half-chestnut which are known in our part of the world as Christmas beetles. 'I found it on the road—a car must have hit it', sobbed its rescuer. 'Will you keep it in your hospital till it gets better?'

I was still peering at the alleged crash victim and thinking of a suitable reply. It lay on its back, looking very dead indeed, but as I watched, one leg waved slowly and feebly like a greeting from a recumbent but affable drunk. The patient was obviously not dead, but that in itself presented problems. I knew nothing about beetles and to tell the truth I had never really wanted to. Thanks to the matchbox menageries kept by my brothers and the uncanny frequency with which escapees headed for my bed, I had never developed any affinity with them. However, you cannot tell that to a trusting young bettle-lover who regards you as the insect world's answer to Doctor Kildare.

In one of the bravest gestures of my life, I held out my hand and allowed the patient to be decanted into it. It seemed happy to be right way up instead of reclining helplessly on its shell like a miniature turtle. In fact, its other legs jerked slowly into play and it appeared to be becoming positively vivacious for a beetle—as well as tickling my palm horribly. Trying not to shudder, I told its rescuer it seemed to have come through its accident pretty well apart from a touch of concussion, and that I would guarantee a full recovery. Nodding gravely, he headed down the driveway muttering 'concussion'—obviously delighted with the new word as well as the favourable prognosis.

I thought that would be the last I saw of him, but I was wrong. There was another knock on the door three days later. He was back to see how the patient was progressing. The last time I had seen it, it was progressing pretty well. I had only waited for the little boy to turn his back before nipping over to deposit it thankfully on the nearest peppermint tree. It had stopped to investigate a tasty leaf, then ambled off along a branch looking quite contented with its new surroundings.

Even so, I felt too guilty to confess the speed and simplicity of this apparent miracle-cure. He listened trustingly while I told him instead of the expert treatment the patient had received; how, after a carefully supervised convalescence, it had been transported back to its own particular tree near the scene of the supposed accident; of the rapturous welcome it had received from its wife and six children; and how it took its rightful place at the head as they marched in single file up the trunk to their nest.

If it really is wrong to tell white lies to anxious children, I plead guilty to being a pretty consistent sinner—even though it can involve me in some awkward situations.

I sinned again a few weeks later when confronted with another woebegone five-year-old carrying a very dead budgerigar. 'I found it on the road', he said. 'Will you make it better?'

Those trusting, tear-filled eyes turned my heart (and brain) to jelly and I heard myself saying, apparently with the utmost confidence, 'Of course I will, love!'

True, I did have the sense to add rather more lamely, 'But it might take quite a while . . .' Even so, he headed home quite jauntily and with implicit belief, leaving me to repent at leisure a promise of which even the Bible quotes only occasional fulfilment. Actually, I did not have much leisure to repent it. Only two days later the youngster was back again asking whether he could see his protege. Trapped by my own deceit, I could only tell him that the budgie was much better, but he could not see it yet because it was isolated in case its 'illness' spread to other birds and animals. This satisfied him temporarily, but, as I should have anticipated, he came back daily to ask how convalescence was progressing and how soon he could see the patient.

In desperation, I rehearsed to myself a story about a sudden relapse, but I just could not go through with it. After raising his hopes initially, I felt less able than ever to face the prospect of telling him the bird was dead. Eventually, pragmatic Archie came to the rescue.

'Having got yourself into this there's only one way out', he said. 'You'll have to buy another blue budgie and tell the nipper this is the one he brought in.'

Actually, it cost more than the price of the budgie; I also had to buy a cage. But that seemed a small price to pay for keeping the little boy happy. I was actually looking forward to his arrival next day, when I could say 'Here he is, look— much better!' and present the changeling for inspection. Unfortunately, I had not reckoned on just how observant a five-year-old can be. Instead of a rapturous greeting for the bird, he put his nose to the cage, peered intently at its occupant and said, 'Why is it a different colour?'

I had fallen into the trap of thinking a blue budgie was just a blue budgie, but I was not game to argue—even though this pint-sized expert had only seen the original bird for a few minutes two weeks before. His face was was already showing disappointment, even a dawning suspicion, and I was close to panic. Again, sheer waffle came to my aid.

'Of course he looks different after an illness like that', I babbled. 'You look pale when you've been poorly, don't you? The same thing has happened to him. He's better now, but he's gone a paler blue—it's all because of hormones . . .'

Fortunately he did not ask what hormones were because I had not, and have not, the faintest idea. They only seem to crop up in TV advertisements, but children are conditioned by those as much as adults and he seemed quite happy to swallow the explanation.

He came back several times, but his interest waned gradually now that the drama was over. However, there was one lasting result. Archie, soft-hearted as ever, decided the cage was too cramped and built the budgie an aviary as big, comparatively speaking, as the Sydney Opera House.

Then he decided the bird—inevitably he came to be

called Lazarus—looked lonely and bought a clutch of companions, widening our responsibilities still more. It was worth it not to wreck the little boy's faith and I still defend my motives, but I have been punished for my duplicity. Even to myself, I sounded so convincing that I have never really been able to trust a doctor since . . .

# Up the Pole, or Anywhere

No one tells you, before you get embroiled in our particular kind of lunacy, that to be properly qualified for it you need to be a cross between a monkey and a commando.

My first intimation of what was required was a telephone call from the caretaker's wife at the Point Walter migrants' hostel, which stood between Fremantle and Perth. It was a beautiful situation, overlooking the Swan River and its swimming beaches, and I had often thought what a lovely first impression it must give to new arrivals from Britain and Europe. However, according to my caller at least one hostel visitor resident was not enjoying the view. It was, she explained, a white corella which was obviously lost and was cowering on the roof of her cottage, being mobbed by magpies. Her husband had high blood pressure and could not risk climbing up there. Would I have a go at a rescue?

Archie was on a police shift and had taken the station waggon with him, but something must be done promptly; magpies are aggressive birds, particularly during the mating season, which it was. The solitary corella, in spite of its cockatoo beak, would have little chance against them. Accordingly, I hauled my old pushbike out of the garage and trundled off on the 8-kilometre ride to Point Walter.

The caretaker's wife was waiting for me at the door, casting an anxious eye upward now and then at the dive-bombing and general racket going on above her head. Those magpies were certainly in their toughest mood, and the corella, cowering on the apex of the roof with shoulders hunched as its assailants zoomed in, looked very worried indeed.

The lady found me a ladder to reach the roof and a pillowcase to stuff the fugitive in and up I went. Unfortunately, the ladder was not long enough to reach the guttering. I had to rest it instead against the house wall beneath, but somehow, spurred on by the emergency, I scrambled out over the guttering and up the sloping roof. There, beating off the indignant magpies, I was able to seize the corella and stuff it into the pillowcase. I dropped the

bundle into the lady's arms then realized that although the corella's troubles were at an end, my own were only just starting. A hazardous slide down to the roof edge confirmed it. Short of converting myself into a caterpillar, there was no way in which I could go out over the guttering, curl back under those wide eaves and regain the ladder.

The caretaker's wife was peering up with her mouth open, having just realized the same thing. After a slightly panicky and abortive consultation, I withdrew my head from over the guttering to reconsider the situation. Since this side of the house offered no solution, was there any hope on the other side? Fortunately, there was. Another scramble across the roof ridge showed the answer to my unspoken prayer—a large pine tree whose regular, horizontal branches should provide a perfect ladder to the ground. True, the tree was about a metre from the guttering, but it looked an easy jump and I was sure my troubles were over.

Unfortunately, I either under-estimated my own weight or over-estimated the strength of the branches. When I leapt out Tarzan-fashion and grabbed the nearest, it bent and then cracked alarmingly. Instead of a neat and even jaunty descent to the ground, I came down like a koala in reverse—clinging desperately to the rough trunk and badly cutting my hands in the process. The caretaker's wife, still watching in awe, exclaimed over the blood and wanted to dress them, but by then I was only anxious to get back home. Putting the squawking pillowcase in the handlebar basket I cycled back to Bicton, attracting a good many curious glances along the way.

Once safely indoors, I untied the pillow-case to let out the pathetic fugitive for whose life I had risked my own— well, my own limbs at any rate. The pathetic fugitive emerged, blinked and bit me to the bone. It chose the hand that was already most badly damaged and to be frank, it already hurt so much that the cocky's bite did not make a lot of difference. However, it was the thought that counted. I restrained the temptation to wring its neck—that would have hurt my hands too—and provided food and water after I had cleansed and bandaged my wounds.

---

This young kookaburra was hit by a car. Its broken wing has mended as far as possible.

We advertised having recovered the bird and within hours his ecstatically grateful owners had arrived to reclaim him, but relations between him and me remained strained to the last. As we exchanged a final cold stare, I could not help wandering whether the magpies, bullies though they might be, did not have something on their side after all . . .

I have got stuck while attempting rescues on other occasions, but the time which got me into most trouble with Archie was a few days before our son Terry was born. This time, the emergency occurred on our own doorstep—or at least in the roadside gum tree only a metre or so away.

I heard a pitiful mewing up among the branches and went out to see a small tabby kitten making a surprising noise for its size and apparently wedged in the main fork. There was no one else about and the tree did not look too tall, so I hauled myself up into it. It was a stupid thing to do at that stage of pregnancy and I was promptly paid out, because the kitten took one amazed look, ran past me and jumped to the ground with no trouble at all.

Unfortunately, the same did not apply to me. I peered down and realized the meagre footholds I had found on the way up were not at all visible from above. I had at least the sense not to contemplate a 2.5-metre jump to the ground, which might have shaken Terry up considerably. Instead, I settled in the fork like an oversized pigeon and waited for a potential rescuer. As luck would have it, it was my neighbour, returning two hours later from a shopping expedition. Anyone else might have been seriously upset at being hailed from a roadside tree. She, having lived next door for years, took the whole thing comparatively calmly. She trotted out a ladder—long enough this time—held it while I climbed down and, tut-tutting under her breath, ushered me indoors for a much-needed cup of tea.

She had a few pointed things to say about the foolhardiness of climbing about in trees when a first baby was due, but that was nothing compared with Archie's comments when he came home. I could only bow my head meekly and endure it; after all, they were both perfectly right. But, thank goodness, it did Terry no harm at all. He grew up to like climbing—and cats.

# Timba and Co.

Not all our animals were wild ones, in the literal or the traditional sense. A mainstay of the whole glorious schemozzle was, from the very beginning, our golden retriever Timba. In fact, he was probably the most devoted and conscientious 'keeper' of us all.

We were a bit apprehensive about his reaction when Nellie, our first patient, arrived. After all, many dogs are pretty possessive about their family's premises and their own privileges. They resent even other dogs, let alone a strange animal that neither looked nor smelt like anything he had ever known before. We all know the traditional human reaction to that type of encounter; even different colour, let alone shape, is enough to provoke aggression. But Timba was a lesson to all of us.

He was obviously baffled by Nellie's many differences and for the first few days we often caught him, quite literally, giving her a sideways look. Far more important to him, however, was that she was weak and sick. He adopted her and made himself responsible for her to such an extent that it became virtually impossible to separate them for long. Timba spent hours each day with his head resting against Nellie's 'hospital' basket so that he could protect her and know immediately when she was lonely or in need.

For a while the little kangaroo was apprehensive about her odd guardian, but she seemed to realize remarkably quickly that he meant her no harm. In fact, it soon became obvious that she was happily accepting him as a substitute mother. Far from being embarrassed, Timba was delighted. He played out his new role to a touching extent. When Nellie's tiny pointed face emerged from the blankets in which she nestled, he would nuzzle and lick her until both were out of breath, but it would not be long before Nellie was back for more.

Long after she became well enough to venture out and explore the garden, Timba retained his self-appointed role as her parent and protector. Soon she was bigger and stronger than he was, but the relationship remained as close as ever. When more kangaroos and wallabies arrived to share the garden, the dog was a friend to them all. He was always at his best though with creatures which were small and weak. I say creatures because his care and affection extended to birds as well as animals. No matter how huge he appeared to them, they all seemed to sense that he meant them no harm—in fact the injured ones were more content and at ease when he was with them.

I remember one scorching summer day when we were both inside the kitchen seeking the shade. Timba was stretched on the floor panting, his long pink tongue extended like a roller blind. Whether Bill, the budgie, mistook it for a particularly tempting worm I shall never know, but without warning he zoomed from his open cage, dropped like a miniature hawk and landed right in the middle of the dog's tongue. Timba was transfixed. So was I.

It was difficult to imagine a more dangerous situation for the bird, or a more tempting one for the dog. Bill was actually within his open jaws with the upper one, like a crocodile's, poised above him. One quick snap would have removed an irritation and provided, in spite of the feathers, quite a juicy appetiser. But Timba was no crocodile. Instead he turned his head very slowly and carefully towards me and looked at me beseachingly as he extended his neck forward and up. I could see the sharp little claws gripping his sensitive tongue and I still feared the pain might cause him to bite the interloper before I could remove it. But not Timba. Although saliva was running from his jaws, he resisted the temptation until I was able to slip my finger between his teeth and persuade Bill to hop on to it.

One of our most prized possessions is a movie film we took of the dog surrounded by some of his many friends. Bill, cheeky as ever, is perched on his nose. On his head is Percy, a white rat, which he had also mothered. Sheena the half-wild alley cat sleeps between his front paws. A lame galah is hauling itself along his back, claw over claw, and all around are joeys of various sizes observing the action with interest but no great surprise.

I have known, at a rough estimate, five thousand animals over the past thirty years, but I have never known one more sweet-natured and lovable than Timba. He died peacefully at the ripe old age of thirteen. I still cannot look at that film without my eyes blurring.

# You Can't Call Your Life Your Own

One day I found myself needing the services of a chiropractor, although I was not the patient.

I had never had anything to do with this rather exotic breed, but a friend had gone into paeans of praise and some impressive detail about a Perth practitioner of the art who straightened her out after she had suddenly frozen into the shape of a question mark while trying to move a full washing-machine. Most of the detail had been incomprehensible, but I recalled snatches about slipped discs and displaced cartilages when a farmer from the northern wheatbelt brought in a beautiful grey kangaroo doe in a very sad state indeed.

If I have given the impression that most Western Australian farmers do not care about wildlife, I would like to apologize here and now. There are exceptions, but a surprising number have both an interest in and an affection for the 'unofficial' inhabitants of their land. Many have pet emus, kangaroos or wallabies which are the apple of the family's eye. This young doe was a typical example. For two years, she had had the run of the home paddock and the homestead garden and lived a life which Riley would have envied. Then her owner brought home a new tractor. The unfamiliar and louder engine note had panicked the doe. She had taken off with those graceful, incredible 7.5-metre bounds which are a delight to the eye, and crashed at full tilt into the high brick wall of the garden.

The farmer and his wife thought she had killed herself outright. Even when they detected faint signs of life and took her to the local vet, the news was really no better. After an examination of the limp, twisted little body the vet said there was nothing he could do except put her out of her misery. It was a verdict which, however kindly meant, her owners could not accept—Joey was too much a member of the family for that. Instead, the farmer wrapped her in a blanket, drove 300 kilometres to Perth and spent another hour asking the whereabouts of the woman who specialized in wildlife nursing, before he eventually knocked on our door. He only stayed long enough for a quick outline of Joey's troubles before starting back on the long drive to catch up on his farming duties. Like most countrymen, he was a man of few words anyway but he was so obviously upset that I was determined to save the little doe by any means within my rather limited capacity. If I failed, I would take Joey to Phil Harwood for a merciful needle and tell the farmer she had died in her sleep. But I did not even want to think about that . . .

I had hoped for Doctor Phil's advice anyway as a first move before starting any treatment, but it was a weekend and he was away. I should have to rely on my own diagnosis.

Joey was lying on a mattress on the floor of the lounge-room where we had brought her for warmth. When I raised her head and slipped a teat-bottle into her mouth she was able to swallow if I squeezed the bottle, but apart from that she seemed paralysed and completely helpless. I was caressing her neck and feeling terribly helpless myself when my hand stopped of its own accord. I had stroked a good many kangaroos by now and there was something different under my fingers—a series of irregularities and apparent sideways kinks instead of the smooth succession of spinal bumps I was used to. I checked a little more firmly just to make sure, wincing at the pain I might be causing Joey, then phoned Joan, the friend who had visited the chiropractor. She was around straight away, delighted to find another potential beneficiary for what she still regarded as a near-miracle cure. To her eternal credit, she tested her own recovery to the full by helping me roll the heavy patient on to a blanket and stagger with her to our station waggon, where another spring mattress protected her from jolts on the way to the surgery.

The chiropractor, in true professional fashion, showed no surprise at being confronted by two puffing women carrying between them a near-dead kangaroo. Instead, he felt Joey over gently and confirmed that she bad indeed got several slipped discs, together with badly torn muscles along her spine and across her chest. The discs were a straightforward matter—he popped them back there and then. But the torn muscles, he said, would present a great deal more difficulty. They would need muscular therapy every three hours—and even if Joey did make a full recovery, it was likely to take anything up to six months. Was I prepared to take this on? It was a pretty daunting prospect, but discovering that muscular therapy was only chiropractor's jargon for massage made me feel a bit better. Then I thought of the farmer's anxious face, and that decided it.

The chiropractor showed me how to massage Joey, downwards from the neck all the way to the base of the tail. Then Joan, brick that she is, helped me get the little doe home and we embarked on a routine which really tested our endurance. I say 'we' because, as usual, poor Archie found himself involved at least as deeply as I was in the consequences of one of my impulsive decisions.

Massaging Joey took fifteen minutes. We worked out a roster—myself at three a.m., Archie at six a.m., twenty-four hours a day, day after week after month ... With a watch-on, watch-off system it was like being the crew of a tiny ship which would founder if we fell down on the job. It was worse for Archie—he had to go on police shifts as well as spend his time at home governed by that relentless clock.

There was the mess too. Joey was still in the lounge-room to gain the utmost warmth. She soon taught herself to open her mouth when she was hungry or thirsty but this was the only movement she could make apart from her pleading eyes, which followed me about the room. I would hand feed her with chopped-up fragments of apple, carrot or cereal but it was an untidy business, especially as she could not be moved outside to perform her natural functions. We put a plastic sheet over the mattress and did our best to keep the mess to a minimum, but the place smelt like a barn. We tried to put on a good face (in spite of wrinkled noses) by recalling the old joke about it being problems like these which reveal who your real friends are. Little though we deserved it, almost all ours stood the test. They still visited, though it was painful to watch their faces turning purple as they tried not to breathe in ...

After six weeks, we decided to take the bull by the horns and see whether the patient was making any progress. We took her outside on to the lawn, where I would stand astride her holding her upright with my arms around her stomach and my knees pressed against her sides. Then I would say encouragingly, '*Jump*, Joey!' and hoist her in what I hoped was some semblance of the beginning of a leap.

This went on daily for another two weeks, several times each day. It was hard work and I felt I was rapidly becoming a chiropractic victim myself when, at the umpteenth '*Jump*, Joey!' she suddenly lurched forward and gave three hops before she fell. The fact that her first hop brought her head up under my chin and nearly laid me out did not detract from the excitement. I ran to her and, after checking that she had not hurt herself, hugged her and crooned to her until she gave a complacent little kangaroo cough and her first attempt at a snuggle.

That was the turning point. Within a few days she was not only hopping away from my arms but was able to stand unsupported. I shall never forget the time when, with my heart in my mouth, I let go of her gently and backed off to see her wobble a little but then regain her balance and look at me with an expression which said unmistakably, 'Look, how's that for smartness?'

We kept on with the massage and she progressed gradually to a stage where she could hop quite well and bend her head to graze. But her front paws still seemed useless. When I put titbits into them, they did not respond. I had to close my hand around the paw and move it to her mouth to stop the morsel falling out. This was more worrying and I began to feel that all our efforts might have been in vain. There is no kindness in rearing an animal which remains partially paralysed and unable to defend itself. Then one day, from the corner of my eye, I spotted Joey furtively flexing and unflexing her front paws when she thought I was not looking. I had forgotten the aftermath of so many protracted illnesses, both human and animal: a crafty little touch of deceit to make sure the attention in which the patient has basked so long and so satisfyingly is not finally withdrawn.

To check my theory, I matched cunning with cunning. When the next mealtime came around I collected a handful of rose petals, her favourite nibble, put them in her paw, closed my hand around it as usual, then suddenly took my hand away. Her paw began to droop pathetically as though

---

A doe similar to the one that received physiotherapy for a spinal injury. This western grey had an injured arm and now raises it whenever Iris comes near as if to thank her for making it better.

to let the petals fall, but instead of moving my hand back to help her, I made a grab as though to snatch the petals. It worked beautifully. Joey's little melodrama was shattered by the fear that she might lose her titbits altogether and she snatched back so healthily her claws would have scratched my hand badly if I had not pulled it away. She realized too that she had been rumbled. As she chewed her rose petals with a kind of sulky relish, she refused to meet my eye—and she never tried her pathos routine again.

We were almost sorry when the time came for her to return to the farm at Arrino, but the joy on the faces of the farmer's family when they came to collect her made the hard work—and even the smell!—well worthwhile.

Incidentally, Joey was far from unusual in her craftiness. The longer I know kangaroos, the more respect I have for their ability to organize humans to their own advantage— often far more effectively than that other monument to self-comfort, the household cat.

I am thinking particularly of another of our patients, an attractive little doe we called Skippy. When she was old enough to feed herself, we gave this orphan to a little girl only a few streets away. That was not by any means the last we saw of her. The following day, a complacent-looking Skippy arrived back, pushed by her owner in a lavish doll's pram. She had come, the little girl explained, for her daily check-up. And daily it remained. When the little girl started school, Skippy arrived looking even more complacent and pushed by her owner's mother, who explained rather self-consciously that Skippy had made a fuss to get out and did not seem to like it when the daily pram-push routine was broken.

On her first birthday, this most spoiled of all kangaroos arrived in one of her birthday presents, a brand-new baby's pusher. She was elegantly attired in a ballerina skirt and lace blouse, plus a bonnet with daintily embroidered holes for her ears to poke through. The overall effect was stunning until she went down on all fours to graze, presenting to view flouncy underskirts surrounding most incongruously a big, bouncy behind. Skippy realized her gaffe immediately. At the first chuckle from the spectators she straightened up, gave us a genteelly dirty look and remained elegantly poised on tiptoe for the remainder of her visit— which she ended by climbing into the pusher unaided and waiting rather imperiously for her blanket to be tucked around her.

We stayed in touch with Skippy who later became a regular patron at the local drive-in cinema. She always insisted on occupying a front seat in the car and accepted as her due the gallery of admirers which always gathered in the interval. I agree with critics who say it is humiliating if not outright cruel to dress up animals and have them behaving like human beings. But anyone seeing Skippy holding court would have no doubt as to whose wishes were being carried out.

# Funny Foundlings and...

Quokkas suffer from a virtue which worries conservationists sick. They are among the friendliest, most harmless creatures alive—which means very soon they may not be.

A chubby, jovial-looking little marsupial, they were mistaken for rats by the Dutch galleon crews who were the first Europeans ashore in Western Australia more than three hundred years ago. As a result, they gave the name Rottnest—Rat's Nest—to the island 19 kilometres off Fremantle which throughout the nineteenth century was a place of banishment for aboriginal lawbreakers, but is now Western Australia's most popular holiday resort.

Farming expansion soon made the mainland quokkas virtually extinct, but appropriately they continued to thrive on Rottnest—mainly because Aborigines kill only for food, not amusement. Sadly, this situation has deteriorated with the white invasion of the island until quokkas there are in need of rigorous protection.

The trouble is not merely that they are too slow to escape evildoers, but that they rarely bother to try. Incredibly trusting and so lazy that they would rather beg for food than forage for it, they will lollop up to every visitor—including those yobboes who cannot see anything smaller and more defenceless than themselves without ill-treating it. There may not be many of these degenerates, but the harm they do is out of all proportion. Their 'amusements' range from beating or stoning their little victims to death, to burning them with lighted cigarettes or flushing them down the toilets at the island's only hotel. As a result, there are severe penalties not merely for ill-treating quokkas but for threatening their survival by taking them from Rottnest without State Government permission.

It was this last law which put me in a quandary when our first quokkas arrived at Bicton. I found a box on the

---

This quokka is one of a pair smuggled off Rottnest Island by an animal lover who rescued them from a group of youngsters who were burning them with cigarette ends.

door-step and opened it cautiously to find two bright-eyed, bushy-whiskered, completely unconcerned 'stowaways' peering up at me. From a letter pinned to the box it became clear that 'stowaways' was the only accurate description. The lady who had left them explained that while on a day trip to Rottnest two years before, she had found the baby quokkas being burned with cigarette ends by a bunch of guffawing teenagers. She had routed the torturers with an outburst of righteous wrath, applied handcream from her bag to the burns and spent the rest of the afternoon looking for the babies' parents. This was probably over-optimistic as all quokkas look alike and quokkas are casual mothers anyway. She had had no luck, so when the time came for the ferry departure she hid the invalids in her picnic basket and smuggled them to the mainland. Then she had taken them home, christened them Jerry and Jane and set about curing their burns properly. By the time she succeeded she was so fond of the chubby pair that she could not bear to part with them.

However, the moment of truth had arrived. The lady was moving to the eastern states of Australia and realized it would be completely impracticable to take her pets with her. Consequently, said the note with more than a hint of tear-stain here and there, could I take over her responsibilities and give Jerry and Jane a good home? Technically, there was no doubt that she was a lawbreaker but my sympathies were with her all the way. The law was meant to protect quokkas—and that is exactly what she had done, perhaps unwisely but to the best of her ability.

Any doubts I had about keeping Jerry and Jane were quickly stifled by a news item about the latest outrage on Rottnest—the use of spear-guns against a little quokka colony there. I decided Jerry and Jane would be better off with us than on the island they had known only as babies. Fortunately the zoological licence granted to us by the State Government meant we could keep them legitimately, but the situation was complicated a few weeks later when Jane complacently produced her first baby, since followed by others. Are the babies legitimate too? Also, at this rate, will Jane and Jerry repopulate the mainland with quokkas? All I know is that our Rottnest stowaways are among our most endearing residents and I would not part with them for worlds.

However, one baby dumped upon us we were not able to keep. It happened to be human.

She arrived after we had gone to bed one night following an entertaining but exhausting day with young Paul, our first grandchild. He was staying with us for a week or two while Terry and his wife Jacquie (of whom more later) were on holiday. Consequently, when I was roused at about five o'clock in the morning by a baby crying, I took it for granted that Paul's healthy appetite was at work and he was howling for his bottle. In fact, he was not very popular when, after hauling myself out of bed, warming his milk and taking it to him, I found he was fast asleep. Grumbling sleepily to myself about false alarms by babies who dropped off again, I had just crawled back beneath the sheets when the crying resumed—but it seemed to come from outside the house.

Wide awake now and a bit apprehensive, I padded to the front door, opened it and peered out into the chilly dawn. In the middle of the front lawn was a child's pusher and in it, howling lustily and quite justifiably, was a baby. Ignoring the clammy caresses of wet grass, I raced across for a closer examination, which made it obvious that the first and most urgent requirement was a change of nappy. Thank goodness Paul was visiting. Not only did we have nappies but the milk I had prepared for him was still warm, so the poor little stranger was dry and fed in double quick time. When she had dropped off to sleep I went outside again for a more detailed look.

The baby and her pusher were not the only unlikely objects on the front lawn. Scattered across it was a varied collection of baby clothes; on the fence were two full milk bottles; and near the driveway entrance was a large cane pram, upside down like a stranded dinghy. It was this last manifestation which really disturbed me. A second pram could indicate a second baby and two new babies in as many minutes seemed a bit much. I hared back inside, shook Archie awake and said without drawing breath, 'I found a baby on the lawn and lots of clothes and a big pram upside down and I'm afraid another baby might be inside it, so please go and have a look.'

It was quite a lot to assimilate and Archie is not at his best in the morning anyway. He was very forbearing really. He said in a slow, reasonable tone suitable for hysterics or idiots, 'Iris, looking after Paul has been too much for you. You must have flipped. Go back to bed and forget all about it.' Then he hunched the blankets over his shoulder and closed his eyes again.

I felt quite guilty about keeping on. When I eventually prodded him out and led him to the door I was afraid it might all have been a mirage and the family's suspicions about me would be direfully confirmed. However, there were the clothes, the milk and the overturned pram. Archie rushed across to right it and, thank goodness, there was no baby underneath it—just a jumbled pile of tinned baby food.

We rang Archie's mates at the police station and the baby and her belongings were transferred to a children's home for a professional checkover. It took a while for the police to trace the mother and it seemed she was not all that bothered anyway. She told them that the little girl was a product of her first marriage, that she had re-married and wanted a long holiday with her new husband. The baby would not have fitted in with their plans and as she knew we took unwanted animals she thought ours might be the right place for unwanted infants too . . .

I suppose there was a certain cold-blooded logic about her solution, but we had so many animals—*not* voluntarily abandoned by their mothers—that we could not really branch out. She was a beautiful baby and I admit I might have been tempted if no better home could be found. Fortunately her grandmother agreed to take her, which, compared with her mother's neglect, provided a fairly happy ending.

Yvonne, the white rat that was dyed pink for a time to make her
more socially acceptable, is being given some flavoured antibiotic on
a cotton bud after having her scratched ear dressed.

Iris, surrounded at feeding time in the sanctuary.

The motherless joeys receive extra-tender loving care and attention.

# Odd Orphans

By now, after a great deal of heartsearching, trial and error we had worked out a reasonably effective way of disposing of our ex-patients and grown-up orphans.

Some presented no problem. If an animal was adult and living in the wild before it was brought in injured, the right thing to do was clear. When it had completely recovered, it must be taken back to its own area and set free there, even though this could occasionally involve a journey of several hours. If they were orphans, good homes must be found for them. There was always a long list of people clamouring for joeys as family pets, but I had to make sure this was not just a trendy fad and that the 'roos would not be neglected or dumped when they became bigger, hungrier and perhaps less 'cute'.

This meant spending a good deal of time visiting every family to try and judge whether they would provide a good home. If I came away reasonably sure that they would, I applied to the Fisheries and Wildlife Department for a permit to allow the people concerned to have a pet kangaroo. One of the Department's fauna wardens would then visit the people concerned to satisfy *himself* that they were suitable. If so, the permit would be issued at a cost of $1 a year. The Department specified that if the animal was neglected it would be confiscated and returned to us. We, for our part, asked that if the animal became a problem or a burden, the people concerned should bring it back voluntarily and it would live with us again. The system depended a lot on trust. However, it worked so well that in twenty-four years only one animal had to be returned to us—and that was not because of ill-treatment, but because of an irreconcilable feud with the family dog.

The last disposal category sounds the most simple— that relating to animal patients who have had previous owners who want them back. However, it can need the Judgement of Solomon to find out just who the owner is.

Big Red was brought to us by a wildlife warden. He was another hit-and-run victim, found lying at the roadside near Kalamunda, about nineteen kilometres from Perth. As usual, he arrived during a weekend when no veterinary help was available. He was a huge, beautiful kangaroo but in a pretty bad way with a severely mangled hind leg. I had nothing to give him as a pain-killer except aspirin before I cleaned the horrible injury and sewed the sides of the wound together. He was quite big enough to have hurled me about the room, but instead he lay quietly. All animals seem to know when you are trying to help.

He was on his feet in the garden within a few days, but there still seemed something wrong. He moved oddly and his eyes seemed unfocused. I called the vet who diagnosed concussion and said there was nothing to be done except keep our fingers crossed. If we (and Red) were lucky, he would recover unaided. He did and became a showpiece of our little menagerie, but an odd thing happened. During his long illness, his lovely red coat faded and changed eventually to a soft bluey-grey. Then he began to lollop slowly up and down the fence, peering longingly through it—a sure sign that he felt well enough to go home. We were all for it, especially as he was wearing a distinct groove along the fence line, but where was home? It seemed a fairly safe bet, as he was found in a built-up area, that he had been someone's pet. Discovering whose presented quite a problem.

A local newspaper came to the rescue by running a story on when and where Big Red was found. When eleven people rang the house next day all claiming to be his owner and clamouring to have him back, we seemed in a worse mess than ever. I resorted to low cunning by asking each caller whether their lost kangaroo had a scar on its leg. Unhesitatingly, ten of them replied yes—including the lady who amplified with a tear-jerking description of how the poor pet had gashed it on barbed wire. This simplified matters because Red's leg had not been scarred until his accident. So I asked the eleventh chap to come and visit us. He arrived very promptly, but equally promptly the anticipation on his face gave way to disappointment.

'It looks a lot like my old bloke', he said after a close scrutiny. 'But it can't be, worse luck. Mine wasn't this

---

Ned is a typical red, with a freckled nose, short woolly coat, and big strong shoulders.

colour—he was a nice deep red . . .'

This seemed to clinch it. When we told the doubter of Big Red's metamorphosis he called 'Karka' and the 'roo came across—even though he had not heard the name for twelve months. Our caller also showed us a hole behind the ear, caused by a vandal's potshot years before, which even we had not known existed. After a cup of tea and a long natter, Karka was loaded into his owner's utility truck for the drive back to Kalamunda. Before they left, the owner stepped back, stroked his chin and cast a fond eye over his pet. 'You know,' he mused, 'when you get used to it, that grey isn't a bad colour at all . . .'

Another of our orphans would have been distinctive by any standards. He was without a 'roo's most unusual and important adjunct—its tail.

Manxie, as he inevitably became known, was a coastal grey joey whose mother, as usual, had been killed by a car. He was thrown half out of her pouch by the impact which had also severed his tail. In addition, crows had torn his ears trying to drag him from the pouch for a meal before a compassionate young truck driver had stopped to rescue him. He looked a very forlorn scrap when he was brought to Bicton. Surprisingly, his injuries healed pretty well, although his ears looked a bit frilly. The main problem was the lack of a tail, which to a kangaroo is very important indeed. When you think that people have difficulty in balancing properly after the loss of such a comparatively small item as a big toe, it is easy to imagine a tail-less 'roo's problems. Not only is it almost impossible to balance while bounding, he hasn't even got anything to sit on.

However, young Manxie persevered nobly. I spent hours each day holding him upright by his front paws, so that he would get used to balancing on his legs rather than dropping on his unprotected stern. It took weeks before he mastered the technique. Then he had to start all over again learning to leap without an outstretched tail to balance him. He fell heavily and often—and all this when he was still so young he was being bottlefed. My heart ached for him but in spite of comforting hugs and kisses this was something he had to learn on his own.

Eventually, he did it. To my delight, he became adept enough to join the rest of the youngsters. He always looked odd, to say the least, but he was a game little devil who always held his own more than effectively. Ironically, he was killed two years later because he had learned to move so well. Frightened by a low flying jet, he bounded across the garden, hit a clothes-hoist and broke his neck. I felt terrible. If he had not been capable of moving so fast, he might not have hit hard enough to kill. But that was silly really. I am sure he would have preferred two good years of life to a long existence as a cripple.

# Who, Me?

The envelope looked so official that I was afraid it was a summons. I could not imagine what for, but I began to feel guilty in advance.

The formal phrasing inside was even more intimidating at first. '. . . begs to inform you . . . Her Gracious Majesty . . . your attendance is requested . . .'

I had to read it three times before I began to gather dimly that instead of being in trouble I was being singled out for a public pat on the back for the first time in my chronically disorganized life. Even so it was Archie, whose police career had made him accustomed to such convoluted official phrases, who finally deciphered the contents of the letter. He read it through carefully twice and then looked at me as though he had never really seen me before.

'It says', he intoned in a slow, stunned voice, 'that you are in the New Year's Honours List. The Queen has awarded you the British Empire Medal . . .'

As a loyal subject, I wish I could say the news filled me with instant joy but, to be honest, sheer terror was nearer the mark. Apart from occasional fleeting and local notoriety when one of our lodgers had misbehaved, I had never been in the limelight—and that suited me very well. Things like New Year's Honours happened to other people —not so much people as Distinguished Personages—whose real, personal existence seemed so distant from mine I could not really believe in them. My own cosy ordinariness had always suited me. Whoever had nominated me for an award (I never did find out) no doubt meant very well, but the whole incredible business threw me into a flat panic. All I wanted was my old obscurity back.

It was this, not lack of appreciation or intentional discourtesy, which caused me to make my first gaffe. I wrote back to Government House in Perth thanking them for the honour done to me but explaining that the frequent and varied needs of my backyard brood would make it a bit awkward to attend the resulting investiture. Would the Governor mind, I asked, just posting the medal on instead?

Iris received a British Empire Medal in 1971 for the work she had done with sick and injured animals. Here she is giving some physiotherapy to a bandicoot with a spinal injury.

It seemed that the Governor would mind. Two days later I answered the phone to be confronted with, 'Government House here'. Then, in a splendidly old-school-tie accent, the caller took me to task and made me see the light. He was much too polite to be reproachful, but there was a faint hint of pain in his voice as he pointed out that although my absence from the investiture might be forgiven by Her Majesty, it would deprive the Governor of the pleasure of meeting me and might distress the mysterious well-wisher who had nominated me. He was quite right, of course, even before he had finished I was feeling both rude and ungrateful, especially over the last point. Full of remorse, I gave my word I would be there on The Day, and we rang off with expressions of mutual esteem.

Then I was faced with the knotty problem of what to wear for one's first-ever meeting with a Royal representative. My own wardrobe was certainly not up to the occasion. Nursing sick animals and fending off hungry ones is pretty hard on durable clothing, let alone fripperies. In consequence, the frippery department had been under-stocked for years. Fortunately, however, friends and family had recovered promptly from the initial shock of my award and no longer regarded me with embarrassing awe. In fact, they were by now inclined to think of the whole thing as a bit of a joke and rallied around with a will to sort out a solution. There was certainly something blue and a great deal more borrowed. By the time I was arrayed for the investiture I could fairly claim to represent a kind of supporters' club. Consequently, I was very nervous indeed, not only about the forthcoming ceremony but about messing up all my borrowed finery, when I fed my impatient menagerie just before climbing into the taxi. My borrowed watch showed me we were cutting it pretty fine.

Archie, looking very distinguished indeed in his best suit and matching tie, handed me in and I sat back in a corner for the sixteen-kilometre ride to Government House. Then I sat up again with a jerk. I think it was the unaccustomed feel of the upholstery that did it, but I realized with absolute horror that in the general flurry a most vital part of my apparel had been omitted.

'Archie,' I hissed quietly, with an eye on the driver, 'I've left my knickers behind!'

For a little while he would not believe it, convinced that

all the tension had either brought on delusions or pushed me into a particularly weak, silly type of joke. When I did convince him, he fixed me with a steely gaze like a prosecuting sergeant and folded his arms with unmistakeable finality.

'It's your own fault—I told you you'd get in a flap if you didn't start getting dressed early,' he said. 'It's far too late to turn back now. You'll just have to go in as you are. Nobody will know, unless you fall over.'

Just the sort of comment to reassure me, of course. I was in a blue funk when we turned in through the lodge gates, up the flower-lined drive and were ushered into the Jacobean mansion, modelled on an English stately home, which before I had only peeked at over the wall.

I thought things couldn't get worse, but I was wrong. I was separated from Archie and ushered into a flower-decked ante-room where the rest of the award-winners were already waiting. The ladies among them, I thought miserably, all looked much smarter than I felt and by their smug expressions there was not a knickerless one amongst them. The Governor's aide, in an absolutely gorgeous uniform, came in to tell us what was expected of us. The Governor, he said, was waiting at the end of the ballroom. When our names were called, we must each enter at the opposite end and advance to a dais in the centre where the ladies would curtsey and the gentlemen would bow. Details of our awards would be read out, after which we would advance to a second dais on which waited the Governor. His Excellency would then pin on our decorations.

The word which had stuck in my mind was 'curtsey'. As soon as the resplendent aide departed I leaned towards my neighbour and whispered, 'He didn't *really* mean we have to curtsey, did he?'

She regarded me with a good deal of hauteur. 'But of course!' she said, obviously having done the right thing and swotted up on protocol. 'Didn't you know? I've been practising ever since I heard ...'

Disaster on disaster. I never had been able to curtsey, even in school plays, and to be frank I was not really built for it now. But the whole thing seemed unstoppable.

Names were called in sonorous tones, the room gradually emptied and far too soon I found myself waiting in the doorway while the lady in front advanced to receive her award. The ballroom, lined on either side with dignitaries and recipients' relatives, was enormous, with a red carpet unrolled along a beautiful but slippery jarrah floor. Just how slippery soon became obvious. The woman preceding me advanced along the carpet to the first dais with graceful competence, began to sweep into a most impressive curtsey, then skidded wildly and only just regained her balance to prevent herself sitting down very hard indeed.

As far as I was concerned, that was it. If such an impressive performer could almost come a cropper on this vice-regal skating-rink, it was a dead cert that I would—and the prospect of falling over veiled only by panti-hose did not bear thinking about. When my name was called, I started down the room and completely ignored the first stopping point. The chap announcing my award did a good job verbally of keeping up with my progress, but I did not realize the amount of momentum I was building up on that long, long march. When I tried to halt in front of the Governor, I skidded and finished up with my nose virtually wedged among the medals on his own broad chest. Previously I had only seen newspaper pictures of the Governor who was a very impressive personage indeed. I had heard that he was once one of England's top rugby players, which indicated a lively youth, but that was thirty years before. In the meantime His Excellency had had a a highly distinguished military career, retired as a general and picked up a string of honours including a knighthood. Apart from size, there was not much indication of the former rugby player in the square-jawed, moustachioed figure which gazed down at me. He looked so stern and the whole situation had got so completely out of hand that I reacted in what my family would describe as typically whacky fashion. I giggled.

The Governor's reaction was prompt and straightforward, as befitted a military man. 'What are you giggling about?' he said.

By now I was past caring. Still addressing his Distinguished Service Order (he was pretty tall, even as Governors go) I explained in what I hoped was a confidential whisper all the tension, confusion and eventual panic that had resulted from my invitation to the investiture. It was like an over-strained dam bursting. I do not think I told him about the missing underwear but it was such a relief to pour out all my woes that I might have included even that. The torrent slowed gradually to a trickle and stopped lamely. After what seemed an interminable silence the voice above me, much more mellow now, said, 'I can see it must have been a bit of an ordeal.'

I looked up to see his piercing blue-grey eyes were now much more blue than grey and that His Excellency, aided by his moustache, actually seemed to be trying to hide a grin. After that, everything came right. We had a muted and cosy chat about protocol and its pitfalls while I gradually recovered my wits and the atmosphere almost rustled with the flapping of dozens of ears on either side of the ballroom.

Eventually he said, 'Well, I had better carry on—lots of other people waiting. But you'll stay behind for a cup of tea, won't you? I'd very much like my wife to meet you.' I did and so did Archie. Her Ladyship proved as chatty and delightful as her husband and I have never enjoyed a half-hour more.

It is not often that I get very enthusiastic about anything even approaching political issues, but anyone trying to turn Australia into a republic would have *me* to reckon with now . . .

# Beetling Off

Our officially approved disposal system for animals which had recovered from sickness or injury was working well, but so was Parkinson's Law.

The more 'roos and wallabies we found good homes for, the greater the number of new patients which came in. Probably the fact that we now cropped up sometimes in newspaper or television stories had something to do with it. Whatever the reason it was becoming obvious that our suburban garden, into which we had squeezed an incredible number of patients and orphans over the past twenty years, was no longer capable of coping with the persistent increase. This forced us to think practically about the future. We had hankered for a long while for a home in the country. With the animals urgently needing more space and Archie due to retire from the police force, now was the obvious time to make the move.

Terry and his wife were all for it too. Our son had inherited our addiction to injured or orphaned wildlife, because or in spite of the first smacking he ever got. I had caught him soaking a caterpillar in a saucer of water—to loosen its fur, he explained, before plucking it clean and eating it. He took the smacking to heart and brought home so many stray dogs and cats that I sometimes wished guiltily that he had not swung quite so far the other way. Then he made up for everything by bringing home Jacquie.

No girl, of course, is ever too good for an only son, but Jacquie comes very close to it. Apart from being an absolute sweetie, she too suffers from animal mania and after their marriage accepted with equanimity, even enthusiasm, the strays which Terry now diverted to her. Their family had recently been augmented by the latest Andersons, daughter Kim and young Paul. Terry and Jacquie were willing to sell their metropolitan service station and pool resources with us.

That sounded promising until we started to look into details. No one had told us that, in the last few years,

76

The Anderson's back garden could not contain the vast number of
animals that came under their care, so after much searching they
moved to a spot in Denmark, W.A., which was ideal for a sanctuary.

prices of almost all country land except semi-desert had rocketed. We went out each weekend to look at properties, but the few which we could afford were hopelessly inadequate or unsuitable for our dream of a real animal sanctuary. We were back to square one, and completely discouraged, when the miracle happened. I suppose the timing was not quite miraculous because a good many of our friends knew by now what we were looking for and were worrying with us about our inability to find it. But the offer was in itself a miracle of generosity.

It came in the form of a telephone call from a Perth businessman, Jack Sheppard, on behalf of himself and his good mate, Bill Maguire. He explained rather hesitantly that he and Bill did not want to butt into our affairs, but they had gathered that lack of cash seemed likely to prevent us from setting up a reasonably-sized animal sanctuary. They themselves were keen on the idea of such a sanctuary, but would not be in a position to look after it because of their own business commitments. Would be we interested in a partnership with them, under which they would help with the finance while we had on-the-spot charge? We could not believe our luck. Pooling resources with our two good Samaritans would vastly widen our opportunities to find a suitable property.

Jack and Bill actually had a property in mind. It was a 105-hectare block at the mouth of an estuary near Denmark, on the south coast of Western Australia. Part was in use as a caravan park, but there was plenty of room on the remainder for the animals. Terry and Jacquie, quite coincidentally, had already talked about a caravan park as a logical adjunct to a wildlife sanctuary and had suggested they might manage that while we took main responsibility for the animals.

When we went down for our first look at the property Jack and Bill had suggested, it was obvious our dreams were about to come true. It was so beautiful that tears came to my eyes. That part of the State is cool for most of the year, so behind the curving beaches through which the river flowed into the ocean were lush green glades, interspersed with majestic gum trees and fragrant peppermints. Gentle fern-clad hills provided a background and there was bird-song everywhere. The caravans were dispersed inconspicuously among the groves of trees, but I was anxious to see the area which had been suggested for the sanctuary.

78

I almost sprinted across the caravan park, feeling sick with excitement. I mounted a grassy bank and there it was.

It could not have been, and still could not be, better. Before me lay 10 or 12 hectares of greensward covered with kikuyu grass, which grows all the year round and makes splendid pasture. There was a natural water-hole, which we could enlarge, and trees to provide shade for the animals. Beyond, the bush thickened into majestic jarrah and tingle-wood trees and behind them again rose the hills. This is it, I thought. As long as we can make enough money just to feed ourselves and the animals, this is all I want from life. I thought myself the luckiest woman in the world and still do. I sat on the bank for a long time before I went back to find the others. They were ecstatic and already deep in plans as to what would go where, including a small prefabricated house from which Archie and I could overlook the sanc-tuary while Terry, Jacquie, Kim and Paul had the existing home nearer the caravan park.

The decision, it seemed, was instant and unanimous. We drove straight back to Perth and telephoned Jack with an incoherent but enthusiastic 'Yes!'.

After that, things became a bit complicated. Terry and Jacquie would be needed pretty promptly to take over the management of the caravan park, so their house and service station went up for sale straight away. Archie and I followed suit, but offers did not come all that quickly. There was a bit of a slump and in any case people looked pretty hard at our substitute for a garden . . . The house was still unsold when Archie too had to leave for Denmark to build an enclosure for the animals. I stayed on in Bicton feeling a bit lonely, although I still had the backyard brigade to keep me company. Eventually, there was an offer which would just raise our requirement for the partnership as long as we sold all our furniture too. I telephoned Archie and we agreed to let it go, even though we were worried about where the money would come from to pay for materials for the animal enclosure. The State Government, of all people, came to our rescue. Some of our friends in the Fisheries and Wildlife Department must have put in a good word. At any rate, there was an offer of $750—promptly accepted!—which was enough to pay for our initial fencing needs.

Then came The Move . . .

# Operation Noah's Ark

Most of our personal belongings were already at Denmark. But the king-sized problem was obviously going to be transporting the animals 400 kilometres south to their new home.

Luckily Terry and Jacquie, who had been caravan addicts for some years, had an old bus which Terry had converted for weekends away. He gutted it of all its fittings and with Archie following in the station waggon, drove it back up to Bicton to collect me and the menagerie.

News of the impending move had already spread and one television station had been in touch wanting to know the time and date. I did not want to be unco-operative, but I was worried about the effects of the upheaval on the animals and I was sure that hordes of strangers with floodlights and cameras would only increase their nervousness. So we decided, if possible, to sneak away undetected. Operation Noah's Ark actually began at night because we wanted all the animals loaded ready for a dawn start to the long and possibly difficult drive.

The trouble was that, apart from sensing that something pretty unusual was going on, marsupials doze until near-dusk and are at their most active after dark. Rounding up the whole brood, watched by interested neighbours, almost exhausted us all. That suburban garden, so cramped normally, seemed to expand to prairie size as we puffed after each nimble occupant to capture and immobilize it.

Our four big kangaroos had individual compartments—crates with padded ceilings and peep-holes, because they are less frightened if they can see what is going on. Joeys were hung around the inside of the bus in the individual woolly pouches I had made for them, each peering out wide-eyed with excitement and curiosity. The younger joeys, which would sleep almost all the way, travelled in the station waggon with Archie. Some older ones I turned loose on the bus floor, together with ringtailed and pygmy possums and other small marsupials. The birds and their mates all found perches on whatever projected from the

This black cockatoo chick was handed in by a forestry worker when
its nest was destroyed during a tree-felling operation.

The Andersons received Pip after her mother had been shot. She was so young that she was still furless and had to be kept in an electric slipper for four months and her body bathed in apricot kernel oil four times a day to prevent her skin from cracking.

walls. Sympathizing with Mrs Noah, I sat in the middle nursing the youngest joey of all—a fresh arrival who was so tiny and dehydrated that she needed constant warmth and almost constant feeding. We were so crowded that one box of the little marsupials known as bettongs travelled on the bus's outside step.

With Terry driving and Archie following we got under way at six in the morning—so tired, fortunately, that I hardly realized we were saying goodbye to our home of twenty-five years. I began to feel sad a few kilometres further on, but nostalgia fought a losing battle against trying to keep the animals in order and thinking of the excitement ahead. Really, they were all surprisingly good. The big kangaroos were the worst, I could hear them shifting uneasily in their crates as soon as we started to move and although I talked to them soothingly they showed no signs of settling down. Eventually, running out of words, I started to sing. The effect was magical. All fidgeting in the crates ceased instantly. So did movement throughout the bus as dozens of pairs of eyes switched towards me and dozens of ears pricked simultaneously.

Terry, wincing in the driver's seat, was the only one unimpressed. He maintains they were rigid with fright or stiff with music-lovers' outrage, rather than pleasurably relaxed. Be that as it may, it did keep them quiet and I had never had such an attentive (and captive) audience. Intoxicated with power, I sang all the way, apart from perambulating the van's interior to feed the animals and one stop to feed ourselves. The drive took eight hours—Terry refuses to believe it was not eight days . . .

I must admit I was almost as glad as he was to see the caravan park entrance ahead. Archie piloted us straight to an empty caravan, into which we decanted all the bus passengers—from marloos and forresters down through tammars and quokkas to cockatoos, parrots, lorikeets, lovebirds and one sick magpie. The only ones left in the bus were the four big kangaroos. I opened the top of their crate, but decided to leave them inside until they were used to lack of movement again. Then I was carted off by Jacquie for a much-needed cup of tea. I came back fifteen minutes later to disaster.

On my way from Jacquie's house I had noticed a beautiful big grey 'roo bounding away among the trees. When I reached the bus I told Archie and enthused, 'It's a good omen. It's not often you see them as close as that.'

'Not such a good omen, love,' said Archie. 'I'm afraid that was Bamby.'

Bamby was one of our oldest friends—she had been with us since she was a skinny joey twenty-two years before. While we were absent from the bus a volunteer helper had opened the door. Only Bamby had bothered to come out and had evidently started to graze peacefully. But when the fascinated volunteer had dragged aside a roll of fencing wire which he was afraid might snag her leg, she had taken fright. The newly-built enclosure had a fence 2 metres high, which we had thought was more than enough. She had demonstrated promptly that we should have to think again, by bounding over it effortlessly before taking to the bush.

It was a miserable end to the day and I was heartbroken. She had never been in wild surroundings before and I did not expect her to survive. For the next six weeks I roamed the bush in search of her, mostly at night when the work was over. I took a torch, calling out frequently and always leaving her favourite snacks, apples and carrots, in the same spot. They were always gone by the next night, but that did not really mean anything. There were plenty of wild 'roos in the area, as was evident from the rustles and thumps which surrounded me on my peregrinations.

To be frank, it was a bit eerie out there in the dark on my own. One particularly dark, chilly night with the wind moaning through the forest, I decided to abandon hoping against hope and go home for the last time. I turned to retrace my steps and bumped into a large, live something just behind me. I am sure my heart stopped. The shock brought me to my knees. I dropped the torch and was left in pitch blackness with the *thing*, which just stood there.

With feverish haste and chattering teeth, I scrambled for the torch and switched it on. There, looming over me, was a figure I recognized unbelievingly but immediately—none other than that dear, infuriating truant Bamby. She recognized me too. She stooped down, put her front paws on my shoulders and held me kneeling while her large wet tongue slurped lovingly all over my face. I hugged her for a long time while I decided what to do. My intention all these weeks had been to take her back to the sanctuary, where her old friends were now happily settled. But, shining the torch carefully over her, I could see that she was in wonderful condition and obviously enjoying her new life in the bush. Much as I wanted her back, it would have been unfair and selfish to deprive her of her new freedom. Instead, I gave gave her a final hug and went home.

Happily, that was not the end. The next night, not really hoping, I took another pocketful of titbits and headed back to where we had met. Bamby was waiting for me. That is long ago now, but every day since we have met at the same spot for a hug and a snack. Over the years she has brought more kangaroos to meet me so that sometimes I now feed a flock of nine. However, she is the only one who comes up to me for a cuddle.

# Acting the Giddy Goat

I do not know what it is about me and goats. They are arrogant, ungrateful, sinister-looking wretches. No wonder the Devil is associated with their image. My childhood experiences with Lucky could hardly have been described as endearing. Yet they still have a fascination for me, although invariably they still bring me bad luck.

There was enough to do at Denmark without complicating life further by setting up a goat. Even so, we soon found ourselves playing, not host but slave and universal provider, to Rusty, whose size in enormous, whose character is infinite but whose gratitude is nil. This is, of course, an understatement. Since he is a goat, he is not merely ungrateful, but looks for positive ways to demonstrate his ingratitude. It was not long before I provided him with a beauty.

He had waited until we were at the peak of our first season on the south coast. We were toiling day and night to get the animal enclosure exactly as the animals wanted it and, at the same time, attending to the needs of several hundred campers and caravanners. Then Rusty, who is usually content to survey any working-bee with a supercilious eye from the top of the wood-pile, decided to abandon his statuesque pose and jump the fence into the camping ground. His looks, let alone his propensity to chew up anything in sight, were not likely to endear him to the customers. Fortunately, they all seemed to be out for the day or down at the beach, but it was necessary to retrieve Rusty before they returned. As Rusty's chief protector in family inquests on his evil-doing, I was elected.

He seemed in a jovial mood when I caught up with him —in fact he didn't really try to get away at all. Instead, he let me corner him, then donned a quizzical expression which indicated unmistakeably, 'And what are you going to do about it now, then?' To add point to the query, he butted me gently. Obviously, it was going to be one of those times. Rusty in playful mood is on the whole preferable to Rusty in nasty mood, but it does have its disadvantages. You feel

Goats have always held a fascination for Iris although her experiences
with them have not been good. After a painful 'playful' incident,
Iris now treats Rusty like royalty—she never turns her back on him.

a bit of a fool when a large goat stands on its hind legs and prances to have his tummy scratched, then frisks around in circles like an outsized kitten. Even if his butts are slightly less boisterous, they can still register some pretty telling hits.

I had coaxed and chivvied the great idiot about half-way back to the enclosure when disaster struck. I was on a mound covered with slippery fallen peppermint tree leaves when one of Rusty's butts caught me unawares and skidded me down the slope with my ankle twisted under me. The pain was excruciating. I was sure I had broken my leg in at least five places. I had to sit for a couple of minutes until the agony subsided a little before I could work out what to do. As always happens on this sort of occasion, there was nobody in sight. The camping site was still and empty. Archie and Terry were working in a shed behind the house about a hundred metres away.

It was no use staying where I was, so I started to crawl in that direction, trying to ignore the stabbing pains in my ankle. What I could not ignore was Rusty. The sight of one of his slaves on hands and knees and puffing hard was too much for both his sense of humour and his sporting instinct. Obviously deciding that I had introduced the best game yet, he showed his appreciation by lowering his head in a mock charge and butting me from behind. That end of me presents a not inconsiderable target. Even though his butts were gentle by Rusty's standards, they kept toppling me over and causing horrible twinges in my injured leg. Unable to get up or move quickly, I had no way at all of defending myself. All I could do was crawl on, tensed for the next butt and howling for help at the top of my voice. Then the two cockatoos in the nearby aviary took a hand. 'Arch-e-e-e! Terr-e-e-e!' I called tearfully. 'Arch-e-e-e! Terr-e-e-e!' those accursed birds shouted, with such exact and mocking mimicry that if I could have reached them I would cheerfully have wrung their necks.

Once again, my reputation for playing silly-asses betrayed me. Both men heard my cries and those of the cockies but assumed it was just Iris amusing herself with the other birdbrains. It was Jacquie who eventually came to my help and even she was in no hurry. She had watched me, she explained apologetically, thinking I had lost something in the grass and had only come down when she decided that

I was not going to find it on my own . . .

Like a wounded warrior I was carried off to bed, where I remained for a week nursing my throbbing ankle and trying to ignore the stifled sniggers from unsympathetic visitors. It gave me a rare chance to catch up on correspondence. However, neither my health nor temper was improved by seeing Rusty through the bedroom window, back on top of his woodpile, catching my eye as often as possible to emit a triumphant 'Ma-a-a-ah!' I treat the beast like royalty now. I never turn my back on him.

If I had hoped for a fresh start at Denmark to gain a reputation as a sane, rational, responsible adult, that hope was soon dashed by the goat incident and killed completely by what followed a few weeks later. It was one of those late-night crises which find few people at their best; I certainly was not one of them.

I had been reading in bed after a hectic day treating new patients and was just dropping off to sleep when I heard a strange, plaintive little call outside. I hopped out of bed, switched on the arc lights we installed to discourage vandals, and peered through the flywire. The water in the ducks' pool below the verandah had dropped to a low level in the long dry summer. Floundering in the surrounding mud and in imminent danger of going under, was one of our joeys. I rushed out and hurled myself into the pool to rescue him, wading up to my thighs in the horrible, sticky black mess. When I thought I could reach him I leaned forward, but at the last moment he gave a desperate heave and a wriggle which took him to one side. I was caught off balance, my outstretched arms disappeared below the surface and I toppled into the mud on my face. When I clambered to my feet and rubbed my eyes clear, I was able to grab the joey who was by then in a pretty bad way. I rushed him indoors, shampooed him in warm water and hurried down to the enclosure to Mousey, his mother. Getting him warm and dry again and back in his pouch, was such an urgent job that I had not bothered to clean myself up. It was not until I was slogging wearily back to the house again that a chorus of chuckles and a round of applause from beyond the fence brought me back to reality with a vengeance.

The night had been hot and most of our customers were

still outside their tents and caravans having a chat and a cool beer. They had seen me, floodlit as effectively as on a stage, tear from the house in an almost negligible nightie, hurl myself into the pool like a mud wrestler and crawl out black from head to foot with my only garment pasted lovingly to me. I had not even had the sense to put something else on before emerging again like some aboriginal Lady MacBeth to carry the joey down to the enclosure.

I broke all speed records getting indoors again the second time, but my audience was so appreciative several of them called at the house next morning to tell me so. As a professional, Mother might have been proud of by far my most impressive performance—I felt sorry I had not stayed in the pool and kept my head under. To add insult to injury, I have an idea the joey's mother did not approve of my taste in shampoo. Being a complete lady, she let me take him out of her pouch to cuddle occasionally, but her expression was rather distant and she always washed him in a very pointed manner indeed as soon as I put him back.

# The Vanishing Pygmy

Pygmy possums are among far too many small marsupials which are on the list of Australian animals so scarce as to be threatened with extinction. If they do die out, it will be a major tragedy. I do not believe there is a more enchanting little creature anywhere.

We met one for the first time when it was brought in by a nature-lover from Glen Forrest, near Perth, who found it in his firewood heap. Only the size of a mouse, they are a perfect miniature of a ringtail possum: curly tail, bushy coat and big wondering eyes. Only their eating habits are a bit off-putting. Their staple diet in the wild is moths, the furry variety, which they catch and pull apart with their tiny front paws.

We had no supply of moths to hand, even if we had been willing to assist our new lodger with its dissection routine. Instead, we sought advice from an amateur naturalist who had focused his studies on pygmy possums and we came up with a suitably finicky recipe for such an exquisite recipient. It consisted of one tablespoon each of cows' milk and Farex; one dessertspoon each of honey and raw sugar; three drops of Pentavite and two saltspoons of Bonox. Mixed with enough boiling water to give a honey-like consistency, this 'nectar' provides a fortnight's rations for a pygmy possum, whose appetite is so dainty it requires only a teaspoonful each day.

Our female thrived on this diet and we were delighted when we reached Denmark to be given a male. It seemed like love at first sight, judging by their outrageous behaviour, but the artificial nectar must have contained a built-in contraceptive. Although their passion continued unabated for six years in the two-storey mouse-house in which we installed them, the female eventually died of old age— still childless and leaving the widower heartbroken. Then occurred an incident which was terribly worrying at the time and is still quite inexplicable.

Another family in Denmark had a pair of pygmy possums and asked us to look after them while they were away on

holiday. Our solitary male having been transferred to bachelor quarters, we put the visitors in the mouse-house and kept it for warmth in a corner of the lounge-room. For the first two nights, I opened the house at feeding-time to be greeted by two hungry but contented-seeming possums. On the third night the male was there alone. I was frantic. Not only was this a rare species, but the handsome little pair were really loved by their owners. What was more, the owners knew that our female had died and I had in fact asked them if they ever found another to bring it in for my lonely male. Would they suspect that their female's disappearance was a put-up job and that I had in fact kidnapped her as a reluctant bride?

We began a search which virtually took our home apart. We took down curtains and examined them, we looked behind pictures and wall-plaques, we emptied drawers and vases—not only at the site of the mystery but in every other room too. At imminent danger to life and insurance policies, we even dismantled the television set. But this was a version of The Lady Vanishes which would have left Agatha Christie for dead.

Eventually—and even now I am ashamed to recall it—my eye fell on Sally, Timba's successor. She was such a gentle dog that even snapping at flies seemed to touch her conscience and on the few occasions we had known her to meet mice she had courteously given them the right of way. After her long live-and-let-live existence with our creatures, great and small, it seemed inconceivable that she had at last displayed a touch of Mr Hyde and gobbled up a visitor. But still . . . Sally obviously sensed my suspicions and was equally appalled at the way my mind was working. She regarded me more in sorrow than in anger; her tail drooped, her ears sagged, she shuffled like a convict unjustly sentenced. She declined politely but positively to fraternize with me, yet somehow she was forever visible in the corner of my eye—a mute reproach to my lack of faith.

A miserable four days followed. We transferred the male visitor to another cage and left the mouse-house open,

---

Pygmy possums are mouse-size replicas of ringtail possums. This scarce marsupial escaped from her cage and managed to evade an extensive house search. Fortunately she returned, as inexplicably as she disappeared, but only after having caused five days of anguish.

permanently stocked with prominently-displayed nectar to entice the truant back if she were still alive. But there was no sign and my spirits continued to sink. The owners were due back the following day and I could not think how I would screw up the courage to tell them we had lost their rare, exquisite little pet. I was so discouraged I did not intend to leave the mouse-house there again. It was Archie who said, trying to cheer me up, 'Give her one more chance. After all, she is a female and they're always unpredictable . . .' I couldn't even rise to the bait, but I left the mouse-house open anyway. I could not really believe it when I looked in next morning to see the dish of nectar empty. I peered into the upstairs bedroom and there she was snuggled into a tissue nest, fast asleep after her mysterious adventures.

Needless to say, we never did find out where she had been, or even manage to formulate a theory. I swear that search would have brought to light a biggish ant, let alone a creature the size of a mouse. She had baffled us completely, and her smug expression when she woke indicated that she rather enjoyed it.

There was a particularly happy sequel. Either her mate promptly forgave her desertion or her absence included a whirlwind love affair with possum or possums unknown. A few weeks later, her delighted owners rang to say she had produced six babies—three girls, three boys—and that we were more than welcome to one of the females. Our widower again became a passionate bridegroom and he and his second wife appear to be living happily ever after.

Sally eventually forgave me and I made such a fuss of her she put on over a kilogram. But it was a long time before I could look her in the eye.

I was surprised, after Archie joined the Force, to discover what a soft-hearted lot policemen are. They may stroll about with tough expressions and a thumb hooked meaningfully into their walkie-talkie holster, but catch them off duty and most are absolute pushovers, at least as far as animals are concerned. I knew it was not unusual for police dog-handlers to keep their dogs after retirement age, but when a mounted policeman almost fractures his bank balance to buy one or two grassy hectares as a retirement paradise for his horse—well, you can see what I mean.

Not that Janniny was an official police animal. He was in

fact a big red kangaroo with a rollicking temperament which would have made him a riot at any police party for needy children. However, he had been unofficially 'on the strength' for two years in a flat in a police barracks before the policeman and his wife, worried about his increasing size, handed over custody to us. They had done their best for him—he was taken for a daily run in the local park—and we arranged to fill the gap he had left by lending them a succession of joeys until these in turn became too big for the flat. Then we turned our attention to Janniny.

He moped a little, but soon recovered and appointed himself our resident buffoon. I have said before that kangaroos love playing to the gallery, but I have never known one who appreciates an audience more. The more chuckles his buffoonery aroused, the more tricks he would think up. He was one of the few animals who really seemed to enjoy the trip to Denmark. His favourite trick is to lollop about the animals' enclosure wearing a red plastic bucket. Presumably he got his head in it accidentally at first, but he found the reaction so rewarding that now it is a habit. He lifts the bucket between his paws, tosses it in the air and darts his head under it like a soccer forward until eventually he catches it upside down. It covers him to the neck, so that he looks like a headless version of King Farouk.

The fact that he could not see did not seem to disturb him until one day, intoxicated by the camper's applause, he over-reached himself. Tearing about at increasing speed to show how clever he was, he lost his sense of direction and landed with a mighty bound right in the middle of the pond. The ducks were highly indignant and Janniny emerged looking bewildered and rather subdued. To save his act and rescue him from humiliation, we cut slits in his bucket for him to see through. He now looks like a medieval knight just starting to get his gear on and plays to the gallery with an extra swagger.

His favourite audience is his original owners. It is several years since they handed him to us and distance prevents them visiting us often, but whenever they do come, he bounds over immediately to greet them. The show he puts on for them as a special celebration is more extrovert than ever.

# Love, Unrequited or Otherwise

We knew the Denmark sanctuary was giving us a lot of happiness. We hoped and believed it was making our transplanted townies happy too. What we did not expect was that it would become a mecca for lovesick rustics.

I was making my daily check on the health of the animals in the enclosure when a big grey kangaroo, instead of hopping up for a nuzzle or following me around, bounded away in apparent fright. This seemed pretty odd, so I did a head count which revealed that somehow we had acquired one more grey than we had the day before. A check of the fencing solved the mystery. At the end closest to the forest we found the tough cyclone wiring, whose lower strands were buried half a metre deep to keep out joey-hunting foxes, had been dug clear and prised up—creating an entrance big enough for an amorous young buck.

Belatedly, we realized what a temptation it must have been. It was easy to imagine the incredulous delight with which this rustic romeo must have come across a previously undreamed-of phenomenon—a paradise stuffed with sleek, desirable houris where food was provided and there was apparently nothing to do but eat, sleep and make love. No wonder, with commendable single-mindedness, he had spent most of the night tunnelling under the fence. Judging by the complacent gleam in his own eye and the warm, reminiscent expressions of several of the does, his efforts had not gone unrewarded. His initial behaviour, it now became clear, was not so much fright or even timidity— more the prudent reaction of the boyfriend attempting to nip out of the window when the husband comes home.

He was a bit of a nuisance really, because to keep down numbers in Bicton all our males had been sterilized— another discovery which must have enchanted the new-

---

Randy (in the background) couldn't believe his luck when he stumbled upon the sanctuary where there seemed to be nothing to do but eat, sleep and make love. He spent a whole night tunnelling under the fence to get in.

comer. The results of his labours soon became apparent and because we now have plenty of space in the bush to release his offspring, he has escaped the fate of the other males. Faint heart never won fair lady and there is certainly nothing faint-hearted about Randy. He is quite tame now and seems not to be resented even by the other males. Watching him cast a kindling eye over his coyly expectant harem, you can see he can still hardly believe his luck!

Another unexpected recruit to the sanctuary is either less bright or less demanding than Randy. She is a beautiful white goose who flew in on our first Christmas Day at Denmark, If that indicated commendable initiative in escaping her fate as a Christmas dinner, her initiative seemed rapidly to run out.

She seemed happy to stay after she had rested, and waddled about inspecting her new home. In contrast to Randy's hot-blooded approach, she selected as the object of her affections a cement swan which poses regally on the edge of the duckpond. Every night she cuddles contentedly up to her unresponsive swain. She obviously prefers the strong, silent type because when we brought in a live and lively gander she would have nothing to do with him, but fled back to the feet of her chosen spouse. She seems happy enough. As Archie says, if the union is blessed with eggs we can always line the paths with them.

A kinkier character is Raymond, our Indian runner drake, whose love life is involved and exotic enough to make most film stars seem celibate. When he first arrived, the nearest resident to his own species was a pied goose. In spite, or because, of the fact that Irene was twice his size, he promptly fell for her hook, line and sinker. His hot-blooded wooing evoked a prompt response and the two became inseparable. Complications began with the arrival of an Indian runner duck. Raymond demonstrated that you *can* have your cake and eat it by mating with the new-comer but still spending ninety percent of his time with Irene.

Irene, flattered out of her mind by this *femme fatale* role, went broody. She was a favourite of mine and, rather immorally, I aided and abetted her by pinching for her two eggs from a big clutch laid by Raymond's real though neglected mate. She was ecstatic and plucked out her down to line a sumptuous nest which Raymond shared with

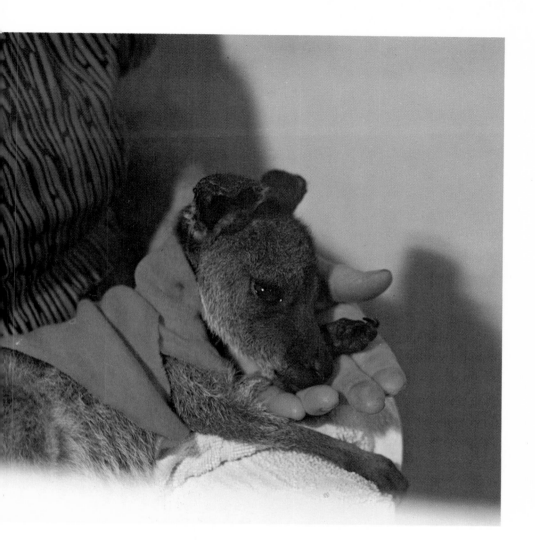

This little joey was taken after her mother was killed. She was kept
in a box and fed cows milk until, close to death, she was
handed in to the sanctuary. Many weeks of intensive care saved her
life.

Mouse's ears are tattered when crows tried to pull him out of his dead mother's pouch.

Midge is a magnificent example of a red euro.

more appreciation than ever. Every night he abandoned his spouse to snuggle up beside his inamorata. Moralists would say that retribution was bound to follow and it did.

Both Irene and the Indian runner duck hatched their eggs on the same day, but crows stole Irene's babies and she was left inconsolable. Grieving for her, I interfered with fate again by taking two eggs from another duck belonging to a neighbour. Unfortunately this duck was a Khaki Campbell and the result was too much for Raymond to swallow. When the ducklings first hatched he was a very proud father indeed. However, as they grew and it became obvious they resembled neither Irene nor him, you could see his puzzlement and indignation grow.

To do him justice, he made no dramatic fuss. Instead, his ardour cooled gradually to lofty indifference until eventually he abandoned Irene completely and returned to his long-neglected but surprisingly forgiving wife. It was a genuine case of a colour bar wrecking a romance, but there was still a happy ending. Irene was so engrossed in her new family that, much to his chagrin, she never seemed to notice that Raymond had given her the brush-off. Like so many human counterparts, she has proved a devoted and contented mother in spite of her flighty past. Most of our birds are devoted parents up to a point—but that point can be a very definite one.

Take our four peahens, for instance. They become enveloped in mysterious maternalism weeks before the chicks are due; they wander off misty-eyed into the bush to commune with Nature and generally extract the last bit of drama from what is, let's face it, a pretty normal situation for most females. The drama reaches its height when the proud mother, having hatched the chicks goodness knows where (we have never found a nest), brings them back to the enclosure for inspection, plus food for herself, before leading them again into the bush.

We used to worry about the danger from foxes, for whom the babies would be appetising morsels. However, we found mum was much too cunning for them. We spied on a family through binoculars one day as the peahen led her brood to a clump of peppermint trees a few hundred metres from the house. We watched spellbound as she gathered the little ones around her, then encouraged them one by one on to her back so that they could reach the lower twigs and scramble up the trunk to a place of safety. Small as they were, they persevered until, with a final flutter, they arrived at a bough at least 7 metres above the ground. Then their mother abandoned her role as ladder and followed them. The whole family snuggled together on the bough—as safe from foxes as they would have been inside our fence.

All of which is completely admirable, not to say heart-warming. The only reason I am a little cynical about the motherhood image is what follows a month or so later, when the chicks are changing from fluffy little darlings into gawkier, less attractive adolescents. At that stage, the mother will bring them back to the enclosure and, suddenly and shamelessly, opt out. One year, all four peahens did their Women's Lib thing on the same day—delivering their broods to me, then heading off with their mates into the bush again without a backward glance for the children they were abandoning. I was left to feed and arrange sleeping places for sixteen noisy, quarrelsome, perpetually hungry fledglings while their parents indulged in a second honey-moon. Eventually, the youngsters were big enough to fly over the fence and forage for themselves. But each year now I have to do my foster-parent bit—and those few weeks before independence can seem a very long time indeed.

One of the oddest pieces of nursing I have ever carried out related to a bird—a pink and grey galah, which are among the best swearers in the business. This one had plenty to swear about. We realized after a while that he had even more of a nautical roll than most parrots and discovered his feet were deformed. He could not stretch his toes to grip a branch and used his beak to drag himself laboriously along the ground. For nine weeks, more in hope than conviction, I massaged those scaly grey feet with goanna oil—an Australian folk remedy extracted from the big, incredibly fast-running lizards which are a feature of the Outback. It worked. Little by little, his claws loosened until they would open enough to do their job properly and Pinky was able to strut upright. It did not improve his language, but he sounded much more jovial about it.

More drastic treatment was needed for a cuckoo shrike brought to us one morning by a Denmark shopkeeper who had found it lying in front of his shop. We never found out what had happened to the bird, but one leg was so horribly mangled that there seemed only one thing to do—carry out our first amputation.

I was scared stiff at the idea, as was Archie, although he would not admit it. We had no way of putting the patient under sedation, let alone anaesthetize it, but it was obvious something drastic would have to be done to give any chance of saving its life. In true Doctor Kildare fashion we got everything ready: antibiotics, bandages, a bottle of Dettol and (it made me flinch to look at them) my household scissors, honed to glinting, razor-sharp edges as best as Archie's grindstone could manage. We decided where the leg would have to come off—quite high to be above the injury—which worried us more than ever. Then, while I held the bird, Archie sterilized the scissors. I turned my head away until one quick, decisive snip indicated the operation was over, without even a single flinch from the trusting little body between my hands.

So far so good. Incredibly good, in fact, but we were still bothered about how to bandage a stump so pathetically small it looked life half a matchstick. However, when we looked there was no bleeding at all so, instead of bandaging, I puffed antibiotic powder over the stump then sprayed it with an artificial skin to make sure it was safe from flies and infection. We laid the bird gently in an 'invalid's cage' with food and water, which we approached next morning very apprehensively indeed. But if the patient had suffered any post-operative shock, it must have been very soon over. He was already on his feet—or foot—hopping about numbly and chirping loudly for more food to replace the ration he had already polished off.

He never looked back. After a few weeks we put him into a flying aviary to see whether he could take off on only one leg, but he seemed to have no trouble at all. By the following week he was so fully recovered that we took him out of the cage and released him. He shot up like a rocket, circled a few times, then headed north—but not, it proved, for very far.

A few days later I was getting the weekly groceries in Denmark when another customer who knew about our sanctuary told me the birds which she fed in her garden had a recruit—a cuckoo shrike, which was particularly cheeky and friendly, but which had only one leg. Oddly enough she lived right next door to the shop outside which he had been originally found, so obviously the place had not retained any nasty memories for him. It was a happy ending to what had started as a horribly worrying case. Even so, I could never use those scissors again . . .

The sanctuary has seen some funny love affairs—not the least being that between a tammar and an agile wallaby twice her size. In due course, the complacent bride brought forth Tammy—a charming cross which, according to zoologists, is not only unique but technically impossible.

Our silliest courtship, undoubtedly, was that between Rusty the goat and a peacock. I do not know who started it, but it was obviously well under way when I surprised them both one day in a cosy tete-a-tete, faces close together and both mouths opening and closing with what were quite accurately sweet nothings as you could not hear a sound.

This went on throughout the peacock's mating season, with Rusty curvetting and flirting outrageously, then bucking the peacock off when it tried to fly on to his back. Eventually, the frustrated peacock lost interest. In revenge the jilted Rusty took to sneaking up behind him and chewing off his tail feathers. They must be more appetising than they look because the goat soon extended his attentions to an emu which was too silly to prevent him. For weeks afterwards, the sight of either bird from the rear was enough to make *us* blush—let alone our unprepared visitors!

# Live and Let Live

When you are up to your ears in 'wild' animals (ridiculous description) it may seem pretty silly to keep the other kind too. I have dodged calling them tame or domestic. Firstly because all our animals have become tame through simple friendship and secondly because I do not know whether you could call a white rat domestic. Yet Yvonne was one of our most intelligent residents, as well as a bit of a show-off.

I must admit I had doubts when she was first brought to us—a tiny naked pink-eyed scrap which wriggled in my hand in a rather unnerving fashion. However, there were blood-chilling hints that if rejected she might end up being used for laboratory experiments, so we hastily enrolled her. Soon we were glad we did. She grew into an absolute charmer and learned tricks so quickly she would put many dogs to shame. She learned to roll over on command, sit up and beg, and wave a paw as if in farewell. Every bit a female, she flirted outrageously with Archie and only he could coax out her *pièce de résistance*—Dying for her Country —in which she lay down and covered her eyes with both front paws. She was cheeky too. She chummed up with Nellie the kangaroo—partly for convenience, it seemed, because her favourite place for a nap was between Nellie's ears, which Yvonne would reach by running up her back.

She patronized our two white cats infuriatingly. We had thought they were black when they first arrived as kittens. Archie, on night patrol, had found them abandoned and almost dead in a coal-pile on a railway wharf. He took them back to the police rest room and gave them warm milk and the inside of his sandwiches, but they were still filthy when he brought them home. A good wash worked wonders and they emerged as two fluffy mischievous youngsters whom Yvonne promptly took under her wing, or paw. She played with them, slept with them and drank out of the same dish. There was one thing she was not prepared to share—her house, which she kept immaculately clean and used most punctiliously, sleeping upstairs and dining downstairs.

Evidently, like a good many over-fussy housewives, she

did not like entertaining because of the possible mess; for when either cat poked an inquisitive nose into her home, she snapped at it so fiercely that they soon learned to keep clear.

In spite of this fussiness and the daily bath which she gave herself in the square cake-tin we provided, we still had visiting friends who shuddered when introduced and said, 'Yuk, a rat! Dirty things—don't know how you could have it in the house.'

It annoyed me and on Yvonne's behalf I decided to try a bit of psychology. I mixed in with her water a few drops of dye used for cake-icing and she emerged a trendy pink which exactly matched her eyes. Instead of yuk, visitors gushed, 'The little darling! Isn't she gorgeous?' while Yvonne preened herself and revelled in every compliment. The dye wore off eventually, but by then Yvonne's new image was established and she had become socially acceptable. Beauty may be only skin deep, but that is obviously the part that counts . . .

Another resident who arouses mixed reactions is Piggy the guinea-pig; children clamour to handle him, mothers are apt to shrink away a bit. But he is a most endearing little chap, a sunny-natured friend of all the world, which is why we decided to impose on him by giving him a lodger. Piggy lives in a cage but stays on the ground where his house is. Someone gave us a Major Mitchell parrot which had been injured. We were short of separate aviaries for convalescents so I decided, for the time being at least, to put her in with Piggy—hoping that as he only used the bottom of the cage and she would use the top, they could achieve a kind of diplomatic co-existence.

As usual with animals, they put their human counter-parts to shame. Far from merely putting up with each other, they became the best of friends. I thought the crunch might come when Chickawee, the parrot, growing more exploratory as she regained her health, found Piggy's house during her perambulations and poked her head inside. Instead of objecting, Piggy welcomed her rapturously—so much so that she abandoned her own house up on a branch in the cage and moved in with him permanently. Now they eat, sleep and forage together. When Chickawee digs her beak in the sand for insects, Piggy is close alongside snuffing them out too. They even speak the same language.

Archie, Dino and Iris posing for a 1978 Christmas portrait. As a pup,
Dino loved to curl up with the joeys in their baskets for a nap.

Chickawee faithfully imitates the shrill, excited whistle with which Piggy greets me when I arrive with his food. Also, I have never seen a more blissful expression than Piggy's when, as he settled for his after-dinner nap, Chickawee soothes him off to sleep by running her beak very gently up and down his back.

One of our most recent recruits is Dino the pup, whom I sneaked in very much against Archie's orders. He had been badly hit when poor old Sally died, and had stipulated, 'No more dogs—it hurts too much when they go.'

I knew how he felt, but it was now nearly a year after Sally's death and I still felt the place was incomplete without a successor. I thought a pup might fill a hole in Archie's heart too. Eventually, I saw a litter of golden retrievers advertised in the newspaper and took the plunge. Their owners lived back in Perth, more than 400 kilometres away, but by coincidence friends from the next suburb would be coming down to stay with us for Christmas. I took this as a good omen, so waited until Archie was out before making furtive telephone calls to arrange that Marie should collect one of the pups and bring it with her.

Then, on Christmas Day, I produced it triumphantly and said, 'Merry Christmas darling—here's your present!'

I was a bit apprehensive, but it was a *fait accompli*. Besides, he could not say much because he had pulled that usual husbandly trick of saying at the last minute, 'Sorry I haven't had time to find you a present—buy what you want.' In any case, Dino was such an appealing infant that I think the battle was won as soon as Archie saw him.

He has taken to the life here like a duck to water and has never chased any of the other animals. Instead, he prefers to climb into the joeys' baskets and curl up with them to sleep. We did catch him once sneaking the milk from a joey's bottle but no doubt, under opposite circumstances, the joey would have done the same.

Archie got his own back when, after a week of watching him exercise proprietorial rights over his Christmas present, I could bear it no longer and pleaded, 'How about letting he have half?' He agreed, but with his usual cunning stipulated the bottom half. I had a messy time until Dino learned adult manners, but it was well worthwhile. And if Archie's end does the grinning, it is mine that wags the tail.

# Bird Brains

One thing I have learned since our sanctuary expanded is that there is nothing feather-brained about birds. It is difficult to get to know those who only make flying visits, but those who, for one reason or another, settle down with us have proved to have as much intelligence and character as any animal.

Maggie is a typical example. Australian magpies are among our most beautiful birds, both for plumage and song; early settlers compared their notes to the nightingale's. Unfortunately they are also inveterate thieves and aggressive swashbucklers when defending their territory. In the breeding season, most Australian schoolchildren get used to ducking away from their dive-bomb attacks. Not that there was anything stroppy about Maggie when he was first brought in. Only a youngster, he had been rescued by a chap who saw a neighbour's children using him as a football after cutting off his wing and tail feathers. Needless to say, he was in a very bad state indeed. He recovered with careful nursing, but not surprisingly took a long time to trust anyone. We did not rush matters, but watched his confidence return as he chummed up first with Yvonne the white rat, then with the two cats. Eventually, when he had regained all a magpie's natural swagger, he extended his friendship to us.

To be frank, he needed a lot of patience from the other animals as well as from us; he was a natural stirrer, at the root of any mischief that was going. One of his favourite tricks was tug o'war with the cats. When I laid a peacock feather across both cats' paws, he would dart in and snatch it away. Eventually, the cats would be stirred into trapping the feather with their paws, often simultaneously. Maggie would then grab the section between them with his beak and tug as hard as he could. The three-cornered contest would often go on for three or four minutes before one contestant gave way.

Another of his favourite pastimes was to dribble a ball back and forth along the yard; with his black and white

plumage he looked like a footy player. But the trick which really upset other residents was grabbing a kangaroo's tail in his painfully strong beak, then hanging on, fluttering and cackling, as his startled victim bounded away.

All in all, I do not think the animals were particularly sorry when the time came to restore a fully recovered Maggie to his natural habitat, although that too presented problems. We consulted Lexie Nicholls (I will tell you about her later) who told us that as magpies have such a strong territorial instinct we should let him go where he had first been found. As we did not know where those horrible children had picked him up, this was of course impossible. We all scratched our heads until Lexie suggested a lake a few kilometres away which we all knew—a magpies' paradise, with plenty of trees and natural food beside the blue water. Paradise or not, magpies are no angels and there was no guarantee that the existing residents would welcome Maggie when he arrived in their midst.

We waited a few weeks until March, when magpies are neither nesting nor mating and, with any luck, would be a little more tolerant about an intruder. Then we drove Maggie to the lakeside and, with fingers crossed, released him. For a while he sat on a nearby bush with his head cocked sideways, watching us with his beady eye and obviously wondering what the game was. Then he flew to a tree branch and, after a few preparatory notes, burst into full song. We sat under the tree enthralled by his music but still apprehensive, especially when, one by one, other magpies responded. First you would hear them singing at a distance, then there would be a flutter and the singer would arrive in Maggie's tree. Soon he was surrounded by other magpies, inspecting him closely while, seemingly oblivious, he filled his throat and tried to outsing them all. Presumably he passed muster because, when he had finished, he and the rest of the choir flew off together. Probably we were idiots ever to worry about Maggie. He was cheeky enough to get away with anything.

Seagulls are usually as cheeky as magpies but with a good deal less charm. Anyone who has seen their vulgar squab-

---

'There is nothing featherbrained about birds,' says Iris. Richard 'Snugglepot', a sulphur crested cockatoo, plays sentry at the sanctuary gate and constantly tries to unscrew the bolt.

bling over anything remotely edible, heard their fishwife squawks and watched their mixture of bullying and cowardice, might be forgiven for thinking them the most selfish creatures on wings. Yet a couple of them surprised and shamed us. Both were brought in with one wing so badly injured that they would obviously never fly again. The first had been established on our pond for a couple of weeks when the second arrived. Remembering how gulls will quarrel and browbeat each other over virtually nothing, we waited apprehensively for the inevitable clash. Instead, the 'old hand' approached the newcomer and inspected it carefully with none of the usual threats and braggadocio. After pecking companionably together, it led the other over to the shady tree where it usually took its afternoon rest. From then on, they were inseparable and almost touchingly considerate towards each other. It really seemed that, hard lesson though it might be, becoming crippled had given them a fellow feeling and brought out the best in them.

In fact, live and let live is the general policy among all the birds and animals of the sanctuary. It even applies to our most fierce and aristocratic denizen—a black falcon, which also has a wing so badly damaged he will never fly again. If he were whole, he would be disliked and even feared; the young of most animals, including wallabies and kangaroos, can fall victim to birds of prey. But he is harmless now and therefore accepted. As he wanders restlessly up and down the enclosure, he is not molested but quite matter-of-factly tolerated—which, to the former mighty hunter, must be the most unkind cut of all.

# 'Orrible Antics

Every now and then you meet an animal—or bird—that really calls your bluff. Edwin the echidna was one; Erica the euro was another; Houdini the emu was probably the worst of all.

We did not have Edwin for long—he saw to that—but he certainly left an impression in every sense. He was brought to the sanctuary by a very harassed policeman who had inherited him from a kind-hearted motorist. Edwin, on a nocturnal ramble, had appeared suddenly in his headlights seemingly bent on a particularly messy suicide. The motorist, having braked about half a metre from his defiantly humped rear, had thwarted his intentions by 'arresting' him for jay-walking and delivering him into custody at the nearest police station.

The policeman had tethered his prisoner to the office desk intending to hold him in custody while his future was decided, but Edwin had other ideas. When the constable returned after a patrol he was flabbergasted to find that the echidna had dragged the massive desk all around the office, inflicting some permanent scars on the nice shiny floor. On his mettle now, the indignant officer decided on sterner measures and locked his charge in the office cupboard. It was a bad move. For a while, all was quiet. Then came a rumble and crash which sent the constable leaping for the cupboard door. His worst fears were realized. Edwin had reached up with his sharp claws and dragged down the shelving plus all its contents. He was squirming on his back with an expression of malicious triumph and with most of the official records either crumpled beneath him or impaled like giant confetti on his needle-sharp spines. His spirit broken, the officer loaded the miscreant into the patrol car and brought him to us.

I was just a bit baffled about what to do with a vandalistic echidna, but put him into an empty aviary for the night so that Archie and I could sort out the problem in the morning. Like the policeman, I had underestimated Edwin. When I took food and water to the aviary at breakfast time, I found he had nudged a huge concrete trough along the soft ground for nearly half a metre before forcing his way through a wire fence so strongly meshed I would have guaranteed it to stop a bullock, let alone an echidna. That was the last we knew of Edwin. I cannot say I am really sorry . . .

Erica the euro had the same tendency to wreck things, although I think her antics were due more to high spirits than malice. Because she was known for her inquiring mind, I never left her in the house on her own. But, inevitably, I was called out suddenly once and forgot about her. I shall never forget the scene when I got back. The kitchen cupboards had been dragged open and their contents thrown on the floor—a revolting mixture of flour, sugar, cereals and broken eggs. Evidence was only too clear that, after eating some of the mess and rolling in the rest, sheer *joie de vivre* had sent her bounding into the kitchen sink. But worse was awaiting me in the bedroom. The carpet was covered in my face-powder, which Erica had obviously tried before deciding she did not like its appearance or taste. The flowers had been pulled from our crystal vases and thrown about—some were even dangling from the curtains. All the bedclothes had been dragged to the floor and there, asleep on the bed itself, was the culprit wearing an expression of blissful innocence. She looked so funny and so disarming that I could not help laughing. When Archie came home he conferred a special award on her—the Gothic Order of the Bull in the China Shop.

Houdini got his name for the obvious reason; he is our resident escapist, if that isn't too confusing. No matter how or where we lock him in, he always gets out. Fortunately, he never wanders far and his objective is always the same—the nearby camping site where he hopes to pick up as many titbits as he can shovel down his capacious gullet. This is fine as long as he waits for titbits to be offered, but he has an unnerving habit of helping himself if they are not. We heard a terrible scream once from the site and raced across to find a woman camper supporting herself against the tent-pole while Houdini busily finished off an exceptionally fine kingfish. She had been gutting and cleaning her husband's catch when something warm and slightly rough caressed her under the ear. Even as she cooed 'Nearly ready, dear', a long, scrawny neck shot down over her shoulder, preceded by a gaping beak which snatched the fish and bore it triumphantly away.

That was bad enough, but Houdini is such a glutton that he sometimes grabs at goodies which are not really edible. We could only apologize abjectly to a very pretty girl who steamed across to complain that his behaviour had gone beyond all polite bounds. Apparently, she had been bending over tucking in the camp-bed blankets when Houdini had wandered silently into the tent behind her. She was wearing the shortest and tightest of miniskirts and the temptation had been too much for the wretched bird. It was not just the shock, his victim complained tearfully, it was how she would be able to explain the bruises to her mother when she got home . . .

# A Double Tragedy

This is an episode which I find very difficult to write about.

It was ugly and tragic and Archie was so nearly killed that I still wake up at night in a cold sweat. Also, through no fault of his own, it did result in the death of Wombie— one of the most gentle, lovable animals we ever had. A beautiful big red marloo, he became a visitors' favourite at the Denmark sanctuary from the day he arrived. In return, he loved and trusted humans; it was that gentleness and trust which caused his downfall.

His first nasty experience came when two boys sneaked into the compound to try and make him box with them. Wombie was twice their size and could have done them a lot of damage. But like Ferdinand the bull, he preferred to smell the flowers and just would not fight back. That was not enough for his tormentors. They went searching in the bush for heavy sticks, then came back and started to beat him unmercifully. A woman camper saw them and came to tell me. By the time I arrived the boys had vanished, but Wombie was in a terrible state—he had a huge swelling above one eye and one leg burst open with the raw flesh gaping open to the bone. We stitched him up, nursed him back to health and thought that as the scars faded the incident too had faded from his mind. But we were wrong.

Many months later, during the Christmas holidays, a boy came to the sanctuary with his sister and asked if he could go to see the big kangaroos. They seemed nice youngsters, so I took them inside. All went well until the boy spoke to his sister. As soon as Wombie heard his voice he went berserk. He covered four metres in one bound and grabbed the boy in his arms. The boy screamed his head off, but luckily I managed to pull him free and to shoo away Wombie—who obeyed sulkily, still rumbling at his victim.

I was amazed and terribly apologetic. Wombie was such a gentle soul that I just could not understand what had got into him. Then the little girl, obviously very upset, spoke up. 'It serves Brian right,' she said, nearly crying. 'The last time we were here on holiday, him and another boy

An adult bandicoot, which had been caught in a rabbit trap, has now been nursed back to full health.

Wombie, a beautiful red marloo, was one of the most gentle,
lovable animals the Andersons ever had.

belted that kangaroo with a stick and made it bleed.' Her brother, badly shaken himself, confessed he had been one of the attackers all those months before. I told him he was never to come into the sanctuary again, marvelled at Wombie's memory and assumed the incident was closed. Unhappily, it was not; the whole nasty business was to be repeated.

Quite a while afterwards, two boys about twelve years old came to the house door and asked very politely if they could photograph the animals in the enclosure. I may have been stupid, but you cannot mistrust all children because of one unpleasant incident. I let them into the enclosure, merely warning them not to wave the tennis racquets they were carrying in case they frightened the animals. A few minutes later, during the washing-up, I glanced through the window and froze. One of the boys was hitting Wombie about the head with his racquet as hard as he could. I screamed at them and rushed out, but they took off like rockets. Wombie just lolled there limply—dazed and bleeding from his left eye, with big swellings already coming up on his head and face. Crying and shocked myself, I gave him a sedative and he lay quietly while I dressed his wounds. He was very ill for a few days, then seemed to take a turn for the better. However, as he got stronger we began to realize that this was not the same old Wombie.

Formerly so gentle, he started to attack the other animals, even the tiny wallabies and the peafowl. He became so aggressive that we barred all visitors from the enclosure. Then he attacked his oldest friend, Archie. My husband had gone in to feed him and when Wombie rose on his back legs Archie assumed it was to greet him. Instead Wombie smashed at the food bucket with one front claw, and with the other ripped at Archie's arm again and again. Fortunately, Archie was still near the gate. He managed to pull his arm away and to back towards the gate until he could feel for the bolt. He drew it and staggered outside while Wombie was still savaging the bucket. White-faced and bleeding, he almost fell through the kitchen door. When he told his story I could still hardly believe Wombie was the culprit. We rushed Archie to the Denmark hospital, where he was given tetanus needles and had his badly lacerated arm sewn up. He was far more shocked than he himself realized. He developed pneumonia and for days he hovered between life and death while we took turns by his bed, beside ourselves with anxiety and grief. Eventually he came good, but it was a long time before he made a full recovery.

Even then, we hoped that Wombie's Jekyll-into-Hyde transformation was only temporary and that if left alone he might recover. Instead, he became steadily more bad-tempered and savage. Six weeks after his attack on Archie he tore into his doe, Bindi, knocking her about so badly that her joey died. We knew then that something had to be done. We could not turn him loose in the bush to endanger other animals and we could not get close enough to give him an injection. There was only one way out. Terry, faced with the worst job of his life, had to shoot the old fellow while the rest of us hid indoors, covering our ears. It was like killing a member of the family and I have never really got over it.

We do not allow unaccompanied children into the sanctuary now, but that does not bring Wombie back.

# Way Up North

Becoming involved with animals has brought us some unexpected bonuses. Among the greatest is getting to know the far north of Western Australia, which I am sure is among the loneliest and most dramatic places on earth.

It arose from a friendship with a couple named Bob and Joan Moore, who brought their pet joey to us because it seemed a bit off-colour. The joey soon recovered, but the friendship ripened and soon afterwards Joan and Bob asked whether we would like to go on holiday with them to Barred Creek, near the old pearling port of Broome, where they had spent their honeymoon. The idea was a bit of a shaker at first. Archie and I were townies by upbringing and had never been very far north of Perth. The round trip to Broome would be nearly 6,000 kilometres—at least half of it over unmade roads and tracks with bulldust holes deep enough, according to travellers' tales, to swallow a car without trace. Even so, the chance was too good to miss so we arranged for Terry and Jacquie to look after the animals and off we went.

The scenery stayed reasonably pastoral and civilized until we passed Northampton, an old lead-mining town about 600 kilometres north of Perth. After that, it was a revelation. I had always thought that the northern outback was pretty dull—just a sandy plain with a great deal of nothing. I could not have been more mistaken. Although we were nearly five days on the road, it was impossible to be bored for a minute. For one thing, there were the creeks and rivers—dry for months in the hot summer, but now in full spate after the winter rains. Only the biggest had bridges. The others just had 'improved' fords—two strips of concrete running across at the shallowest point. If the wheels slipped off them you were in real trouble and with the water pushing and gurgling against the upstream side of the car, it was anything but easy to steer a straight course.

Then there were the hills; not all that big, certainly, but the oddest shapes I had ever seen. Some are like the mesas and buttes in cowboy films; flat-topped plateaux showing how high the sea had reached millions of years ago. Some have eroded away leaving an old volcanic core or plug sticking up like a cherry on a cake. Others still are so opulently curved they look really sexy. One twin peak near the iron-ore mining town of Tom Price is called Mount Bardot—and it was not hard to see why . . .

Even the level spinifex plains were full of interest. The baked soil is almost blood-red, and the scrub and spiky bushes hide a wealth of wild life—emus, kangaroos, dingoes and foxes, as well as the tough looking sheep and cattle that are rounded up by aboriginal station-hands only once a year. This was the area where so many of our traffic-bashed patients had come from and we were sad to see a lot of dead 'roos along the road. We checked each pouch for joeys, but fortunately there were none. This near-desert had plenty of bird-life too—great flocks of corellas being preyed upon by fierce little hawks. The hawks were very cunning indeed. Because there are no trees for about 200 kilometres, they had built their untidy nests on the best vantage points—the telegraph poles which run by the side of the only road.

The nights were wonderful. I had read, and disbelieved, stories about the stars looking so close you could touch them, but it really is true. I would lie for hours, just staring up at the jewelled velvet sky and listening to the not very melodious howls of distant dingoes, before I crawled into the tent and went to sleep.

I did find a few snags one night—quite literally. In fact there were more than a few. Feeling a seasoned outback hand, I spread my blanket on the ground, sprawled out on it and leapt up again very smartly indeed. The blanket concealed a big patch of doublegees, or caltrop weed—a nasty little plant with multi-spiked seeds so designed that, however the seed lies, at least one spike sticks straight up. I had impaled myself on a couple of dozen, whose spikes had broken off in me when I moved so quickly. Archie spent the next hour removing them from some pretty embarrassing places.

---

This little orphan, with unusual facial markings, is one of many which come to the sanctuary after their mothers have been run down by cars. The Andersons always check the pouches of dead kangaroos they see by the road to make sure there is no joey inside.

Next day we had our first encounter with a wild camel, except that he was not wild enough. Embarrassingly friendly in fact, not to say pushy. Camels have been a feature of the outback for more than 100 years and are largely responsible for opening it up. The early pioneers realized that, with their ability to go without water and eat almost anything, they were an ideal pack animal for this inhospitable terrain. Camel trains and their Afghan drivers were a familiar sight well within living memory, until the train and the motor truck took over. The Afghans' descendants are now respectable city dwellers, but the camels took to the bush and, like good migrants, raised families with almost embarrassing enthusiasm. For better or worse, they seem to be here for good.

The first we met was 1,500 kilometres north of Perth at Whim Creek, once a copper-mining township, now just a single pub at the side of the dusty track. It had been a long, dry drive that morning, Bob and Archie were out of the car and into the bar before Joan and I could disentangle even one leg from the bundles which always seem to pile up behind the front seats. It was then, from the direction of the Gents, that the camel appeared. We learned later that he was a kind of mascot who never strayed far from the pub and had developed a taste and a thirst for beer which had earned him the ungrudging respect of the locals.

On this occasion he had evidently been treated to cans of lager all morning. He was visibly staggering a little, but that did not prevent him breaking into a shambling run in our direction as soon as Joan and I got out of the car. Close up, a camel is very big indeed. I had no hesitation in leaping back inside and winding up the car window, with Joan only a fraction behind me. However, as an old northern hand she was determined not to be too intimidated. Instead of closing her window, she opened a tin of biscuits and nonchalantly passed one to the camel. This proved to be a mistake. Before we knew it, we were joined inside the car by 3 metres of neck and an enormous head with rows of yellow teeth and breath that would stun a horse. Pinned inside, all we could do was placate the brute with biscuits and wait until Bob and Archie got back from the bar. That seemed hours, and probably was. All our lunch had disappeared down that unbelievably long gullet before our menfolk re-emerged blinking into the sunshine, wearing woozy expressions which, on reflection, were rather like the camel's.

Even then, they were in no hurry to help us. In fact they seemed to think our plight rather funny and stood off grinning like idiots while we screamed at them to lift the siege. Instead, Bob suddenly sprinted for the car and hurled himself in through the driver's door, which was on the opposite side to the camel. That left Archie outside on his own, with a guffawing Bob (so much for all that mateship business!) threatening to drive off and leave him unless he hurried up. Put on his mettle, Archie strode up to the camel, tapped it on the rump, then put his shoulder against it and heaved. Not much happened for a while. He shoved and puffed, getting steadily redder, while we watched awe-struck at his audacity. Then the camel moved—but not in the way he expected. Instead, it backed smartly clear of the window, almost trampling Archie underfoot, then turned with a very nasty expression and chased him around the car. Archie was on his fourth lap and visibly losing ground before Joan, bless her, recovered her wits and tossed the biscuit tin through the window. The camel stopped for only a moment to check that it was empty, then gave it a kick any footballer would have envied. That gave us just long enough to haul Archie into the car and get away to a racing start.

Men are funny. Instead of having a go at Bob about his heartlessness, Archie joined him in his chuckles. They both fell about laughing so much we thought they would crash the car. Archie had only one complaint. All that sprinting, he said, had made him so thirsty he needed another visit to the pub . . . He didn't get it.

Wild donkeys were the next hazard on the long road north, then wild goats, kangaroos and emus in such quantities that we really had to hold down the speed of the car to avoid all these mobs of jaywalkers.

Emus were the worst. You would see a bunch of them standing at the verge with heads nodding and turning, exactly like old ladies having a very confidential gossip. Then, as we approached, they would all suddenly rush into the road, scuffing up clouds of dust and their huge bustles bobbing comically. The trouble is that both the bird and the car would be badly damaged if you hit one. As Bob said, emus are a bit big to play chicken . . .

Wild turkeys seem much more intelligent. For one thing, they lay only one egg a year and spend the rest of the time stalking about with intellectual expressions. Their proper (or improper) name is bustard, but they look so superior I would never dare to call them it.

Add flocks of multi-coloured parakeets, doves and budgerigars, millions of wildflowers from skyblue delphiniums to the dramatic scarlet sturt pea, and the trip became a kaleidoscope of never-ending delight. People are so rare up there that even the snakes do not seem shy. We pulled up when we saw a black-headed python weaving across the road and got out to have a look. It was easy to see he had just shed his skin, for he was absolutely gorgeous; body resplendent in tones ranging from cream to azure blue and head shining as though it had just been dipped in black enamel. He was not at all upset and stayed to bask in our admiration before gliding off through the scrub.

Only one thing saddened me as we cleared the 500 kilometres of never-never north of Port Hedland and approached the station country near Broome; the number of skeletons of horses and cattle. Somehow, even the toughest domesticated animals do not seem able to cope with outback life as well as those whose ancestors have lived there for tens of thousands of years. It became obvious why there were so many eagles and kestrels in the area—and why they were so fat . . .

No wonder Joan and Bob were keen to get back to Barred Creek. We arrived there just as the sun was setting and it was an absolute paradise—a calm lagoon brimming with cool, clear water patterned with the leaves of water-lilies. I waffled ecstatically about how marvellous our first swim would be next morning, not getting the point of the grins exchanged between Bob and Joan. However, it became obvious when I wriggled into my bathers next morning and raced for the lagoon all ready to dive in. It was a good job I didn't. Instead of all that lovely water, I found myself on the edge of a 10-metre drop with nothing at the bottom except gooey, greasy mud. Out of it grew mangrove trees—the tops of which were the 'lily leaves' I had admired the night before. Barred Creek was well and truly tidal—and the tides of north-western Australia have about the greatest rise-and-fall anywhere in the world . . .

Even so, Barred Creek did prove to be fascinating. With the tide in, it was plenty deep enough for pearling luggers—in fact they used it often in the early days. With the tide out, it became a haunt for thousands of wading birds like jabirus, while the surrounding trees were loaded with cockatoos and corellas—it looked as if they were in perpetual blossom. One thing I did not like was the enormous mangrove crabs over half a metre across which swarmed at low water. They really gave me the creeps, especially after dark. However, they have not stopped the four of us going back—twelve times to be exact, which has added up to an awful lot of kilometres. There is one difference. We are older now and a bit better off and we have given up the tent for a nice big caravan. The men like it because it has a fridge to keep the beer cold. I like it because it is well clear of the ground and not even the most determined mangrove crab could possibly get in!

# Dedicated Friends

Even better than introducing us to new and fascinating places, being animal lovers has resulted in us meeting other wildlife addicts from all parts of the world. It is amazing who finishes up in our kitchen, swapping stories of pets, patients and sometimes downright pests.

Among these friends is a girl whose devotion to injured birds has become a life's work—Lexie Nicholls, of Dalkeith, a suburb of Perth. With her mother's help, she began taking in hurt and stranded birds when only a teenager. As her nursing skill became known, more and more people brought feathered patients to her and her home has been virtually a bird hospital for more than twenty years.

Her greatest achievement was helping to save from extinction one of the world's rarest birds, the Noisy Scrub Bird, a shy, rather drab-looking little creature which makes up for its lack of dramatic plumage by the sheer strength of its song. It was discovered by naturalist John Gilmore near the south coast in 1842, only thirteen years after the first white settlers arrived in Western Australia. It was always scarce and after the last reported sighting in 1889 it was believed to have died out. Then, seventy-two years later, it was re-discovered at Two People Bay, east of Albany.

The news caused such excitement among ornithologists that the Duke of Edinburgh, who is a very keen bird-watcher, went down himself to have a look while he was visiting Western Australia. The area had been chosen for a new townsite, but to protect the tiny colony of noisy scrub birds the plans were changed and it was declared a special reserve. However, there were so few birds that they were still in danger of becoming extinct. To prevent this, the Commonwealth Scientific and Industrial Research Organization decided to try and capture some chicks and encourage them to breed safely in captivity so that more

---

Paula, a black lamb which walks on her hind legs and shakes hands, was a gift from visitors to the sanctuary.

colonies could be founded. When, after a lot of effort, the CSIRO captured its first chick, Lexie Nicholls was entrusted with the job of rearing it.

It was a tremendous responsibility. The baby bird was only eighteen days old and no one knew anything about its food or behaviour. Lexie drew on her knowledge for an 'infant diet' that seemed to work, but the chick needed feeding every ten minutes or so for thirteen hours a day. After two months Lexie went down with a bad dose of influenza, but she moved her bed into the same room as the baby and made sure that its life was never endangered by missing a meal. There was quite a problem over weaning it. It went into moult and seemed in danger of dying and although Lexie obtained termites and cockroaches from its native area it refused to eat from a bowl. A naturalist friend came to the rescue and suggested the termites and mealworms should be put in a coffee jar lid, then covered with vinyl leaves to simulate a natural feeding environment. When the chick saw the leaves it flipped them back, discovered the insects and gobbled them up happily. But Lexie's job was not over. When the chick was old enough to be transferred to the CSIRO's wildlife division premises, she went with it and slept in an observation room next to its cage so that it would not fret. Lexie lost a lot of weight over that first noisy scrub bird, but she has since reared several others successfully for the CSIRO colonization project. If the plan does work, she deserves most of the credit.

We have lots of other animal-addict friends including Tom Spence, the curator of South Perth Zoo, who has given a great deal of help and advice. Probably our greatest surprise was an entirely unexpected visit, when we were still living in Bicton, from someone I had always longed to meet—the chap who always makes me laugh with his animal books, Gerald Durrell. I did not even known he was in Western Australia but when that beaming, bearded face turned up at the door I recognized it immediately. With him were his wife Jacquie, their secretary Anne and Lady Sarah Calthorpe, another keen conservationist.

I was pretty embarrassed at first as I was in my scruffy gardening gear and was not even wearing shoes, but I need not have worried. They took their shoes off too and we all sat on the lawn swapping stories while the nosiest of our

One of the animals that came up to be introduced to Gerald Durrell
was Tammy, called a Tamagile by the Andersons as she is a cross
between a tammar and an agile wallaby from the Leopold Ranges.

birds and animals wandered up to be introduced.

It was a wonderful morning; I learned a lot and I was really sorry to see them go. A few weeks later, after the Durrells had got back to their zoo in the Channel Islands, I received a lovely letter and a cheque for $500 to help Archie and I carry on with our animal welfare work. I was flabbergasted! This was a complete surprise and in fact I wondered whether to send it back. That might have seemed ungracious, though, so instead I used it to start a rescue fund for immature and abandoned animals and birds. With the fund, we have been able to buy medical supplies and books explaining how to care for injured creatures scientifically, including the proper setting of badly broken limbs. Thanks to the fund, we are a good deal more professional now than we used to be. Our biggest project is a proper animal clinic. If we succeed in achieving it, the invitation to officially open the clinic will go to the friend mainly responsible for the idea—Gerry Durrell.

# The Best Place to End

I am in the little glade which has been a daily rendezvous for Bamby and I ever since she jumped the sanctuary fence and took to the wild nearly five years ago. It is enchanted territory. In the foreground is deep grass of an unbelievable glowing green, from which spring the long graceful stems and fuzzy green-and-black heads of kangaroo paws, Western Australia's State Flower. Forming a backcloth are the gnarled, twisted trunks of banksia trees. Between them, like a natural garden, grow blossoming shrubs of several kinds, so that there is colour throughout the year. The small pool nearby is fringed with twittering birds. They fall silent when I appear, but begin to sing and chatter again when they realize I am a familiar intruder. As I sit waiting, four rabbits edge out of their burrows and inspect me with twitching noses and big dark eyes. They scatter as Bamby appears through the trees with two companions. They keep their distance, but Bamby lollops slowly up to me to take the apples and carrots I hold out to her.

She munches deliberately and with relish, staring vacantly into space. I wonder what her thoughts are. She is twenty-five years old now, a stately dowager past bearing joeys. Even so, I saw her yesterday washing the little ones of her wild mates. Can she remember the old, crowded days at Bicton? She is so much better off here—no hunters, but with complete freedom in one of the loveliest environments imaginable. It is a peaceful, mellow, beautiful setting in which to grow old; for Archie and me too.

The carrots and apples are finished. Bamby, after a questioning look at me, rejoins her friends and all three fade away into the green gloom beyond the banksias. It is late afternoon now and the sun is sinking. The shadows lengthen and deepen, but they are friendly shadows, not frightening. The birdsong is fading drowsily. Soon silence falls; complete, peaceful, unspoiled by raucous engines or waffling television.

I cannot think of a better place to end.